THINK LIKE A LENDER

The Small Business Owner's Guide for Getting Loans, Credit &
High Limit Funding Love

Monique Parsons

To my Mario... my business partner extraordinaire, and the man who funds me with the gift of patience, encouragement and the most delicious breakfast tacos of every possible configuration. Thank you for always supporting me. You're the best.

And to my brilliant and beautiful Layla... This book lives and breathes because of you. You are the stuff that daughter dreams are made of. Go forth and be (even more) amazing.

Contents

Yeah, you need this book!

"The rich focus on return on investment, while the poor focus on return on effort."

— **Monique Parsons, author**

I've been solopreneuring online since 1992... a year before the web even came into existence! Back then I was on CompuServe and FTP and Gopher, amazed at what I was seeing. I knew that I'd make a fortune online -- and I have.

I've spoken on stages from coast-to-coast. I had my own radio show. I've taught online business at the collegiate level. I've ghostwritten enough content that you could probably build a house with it all. I've developed software. I've built and sold profitable websites. I've started retail shops both on and offline – (yup, I've done Etsy, Amazon and eBay baby!)

And yes, just like any long-term entrepreneur, I've had a couple of really spectacular failures. The last one I had back in 2008 decimated my emotional and financial well-being for a long time. A very long time.

There were quite a few mistakes I made back then. Not being active on social media was one of them. Not paying attention to my cashflow was another. But screwing up my credit. Man! That was the wildcard I didn't anticipate would be the kick in the head.

The fallout of losing a business that I'd invested six-figures into... along with being a single mom AND having insanely bad credit, was a lot. I never told friends and family how intense it was back then, but it was a serious dark night of the soul.

When I regained my footing, one of the first things I focused on was my credit. Having bad credit for so many years hindered me in ways I could never imagine.

Having bad credit meant that I had to put down a bigger deposit to get an apartment. It meant that I had to put down a big deposit to get my utilities turned on. Everything, everything, everything costs more with bad credit.

And that's why I teach what I teach in this book and on the Funding Preppers website.

I didn't come from a household where we spoke about credit. And while the internet is full of credit resources today, it wasn't like that back in the 90's when I was younger and trying to find my financial footing.

Don't get me wrong, I always had cash in the bank. But I did not understand the value of holding on to my cash and letting the bank fund my ideas.

Always remember this...

The bank is using your money to make more money.

That's what they do. Banks don't sell lemonade to pay interest on your savings account. They sell your money to others, and pocket most of the interest.

That's their great big business model – and I'm not mad.

But this is also why I don't hesitate to reverse UNO that card and use their money to grow my own business.

While the middle class is walking scared, rich people are Usain Bolting 10 burger joints across your state, using a little bit of their money and a whole lot of yours.

I don't make the rules. I just understand how the game is played, and I do everything to stay on the winning side.

So yeah, in a roundabout, nutshell kind-of-way, that's how I became a champion of maintaining good credit, a funding strategist, and the author of Think Like a Lender.

I believe in the value of cheap debt.

Cheap debt is like insurance. I get to keep my money and grow my business, and it's literally costing me pennies on the dollar for that luxury.

I understand the power of having an idea on Monday and being able to launch the business on Friday, while keeping 100% equity.

We launched our transportation business in 12 days flat. The week we started that business, we were making money. And the whole operation was funded – from the LLC, to the DOT, to the F-250.

That's the power of funding.

I'm not here to tell you to bite off more than you can chew.

I understand that I have a lot more 'in the trenches' business experience than most people.

Still, this is what I wish I would've known 30 years ago. I wish I would've understood and took advantage of funding a lot sooner in my solopreneur career.

I've had so many missed opportunities because I didn't understand that there was another way to grow my business.

Let my mistakes be the wind beneath your wings.

And let this book be compass you need to find your way to the treasure chest.

INTRODUCTION

The #1 Thing Guiding a Lender's Decision

Whether you're face-to-face with a lender, talking to them on the phone, or applying online, lenders want to know three key things about you before they're willing to provide you with a loan, line of credit, or even a credit card:

1. **Do you have the financial capacity to repay a loan?** In other words, do you make enough money to repay a loan? Does your income comfortably support the terms of a new debt?

   If you're asking for a $50,000 business loan, and your business is bringing in $63,000 a month, it absolutely looks like you can afford to take on the loan. You submit your application and start making plans for what you're going to do with the money.

   One hour later – application denied!

   That's because out of that $63,000 a month, $26,000 goes to rent for the storefront... $8,000 goes to paying your employees... $19,000 goes to credit card debt... and $8,500 goes to taxes... leaving you with $1,500.

   Do you reeeeeally have the bill juggling skills to add a $50,000 loan to the mix? NOPE, you don't!

2. **Will that cash source continue?** Lenders want to know that your income is consistent.

    If you have a job, you get a paycheck every week, every other week, or every month. That's consistent income.

    Lenders want to see that same kind of consistency if you run a business. That consistency may take the form of daily Stripe or PayPal deposits in your business bank account. Maybe it's monthly deposits from Amazon or checks from clients.

    Either way, they want to see that you have a history of being paid, and that your income is above a certain level.

3. **Are you *willing* to pay the loan?** Everyone says they're willing to pay a debt when they want it. However, lenders use your credit report as the real truth serum.

    If you have a late payment on your Visa in January, then another late payment on your mortgage in April, and a charged-off Mastercard from 2021, leading to an unpaid $2,899 collections account, you don't exactly look like a shining debt paying star.

    Even worse is when you make the money to repay a debt, ignore the debt anyway, and then visit the funding table to secure another bag.

And that leads me to the #1 thing guiding all lending decisions – RISK.

Absolutely nothing happens until risk is assessed. When lenders are looking at your credit report, your credit scores, and other financial documents, they're ultimately using all that data to determine how risky it is to lend to you.

It's the same whether you're applying for a subprime secured credit card or a $250,000 loan. Risk is the judge and jury across every single funding product.

Every lender has a certain level of risk they're willing to take

Some banks, like Capital One, are willing to give a credit card to almost anyone -- even if you've previously defaulted with them. They don't mind taking on consumers with fair-to-bad credit. That's their primary niche.

On the flip side, when a lender takes on that much risk, it creates unique consequences for consumers who use their products.

For example, Capital One is well known for severely limiting how much credit they'll give you. You could be making $200,000 a year, with paystubs as proof, and Capital One will shrug their shoulders and keep your Quicksilver card at $750 forever.

Furthermore, they make a lot of money off the interest when consumers don't pay the bill in full every month. Not surprisingly, the interest rates on their credit cards can be sky high.

Capital One is also very willing to sue consumers who default on their cards. In fact, a study by ProPublica revealed that Capital One was the #1 filer of debt collection lawsuits across 11 states. Most credit card companies sell their delinquent accounts to debt collectors, but not these guys! They are one of the few credit card companies that will sue you themselves.

I'm not trash talking Capital One because of their practices. An overpriced responsibility is still a responsibility when you sign a contract. And if you don't pay your debts, you run the risk of being sued. It's nothing personal.

I just want you to see how risk is guiding their business. Capital One takes on an extraordinary amount of risk, and the repercussions of that trickles down to consumers.

Other banks, like Chase, are far more selective about who they give money to.

I have a great credit profile, and I can't get a Chase credit card. They'll automatically decline you if you have more than five new accounts within a 24-month period. (That's me!)

Chase realizes that there are certain risks with consumers who take on more than five new credit card accounts in a two-year timeframe.

Until recently, I couldn't get a Bank of America credit card because of an overdrafted checking account I had with them more than 25 years ago.

Even though I've been able to get all kinds of loans, business credit, credit cards and lines of credit, certain banks still consider me a high risk. The good thing is, I know this!

Over the years, I've studied a shockingly high number of banks and lenders. I've learned what makes them say "yes" to a funding request. I've learned what makes them say "no." I have a grasp on what their risk levels are, and I've deliberately built my credit profile to be of minimal risk.

The strategies you're about to learn in this book, helped me get upwards of $90,000 just in credit cards, within a year of me putting it into action. Since then, I've also been able to secure multiple loans, lines of credit, and of course, even more credit cards.

In that time, I've learned that to minimize how risky you appear to lenders, you have to set your sights way beyond a three-digit credit score. Depending on the lender, there may be MANY elements they'll take into consideration before approving you for funding.

Most people don't know what those elements are - but I do. And soon, you will too. That's what Think Like a Lender is all about.

When you think like a lender, you'll start viewing your financial actions in terms of how risky they are. You'll know how to minimize risk, ultimately making you denial proof.

This is all born from a lifetime of business experience

B efore we begin this deep dive, allow me to introduce myself. My name is Monique Parsons. I'm a small business credit and funding strategist, based out of Miami, Florida.

My superpower is that I've been on both sides of the funding desk.

As a funding strategist, I help small business owners get the money they need to start and grow successful businesses. I work with several lenders and financial institutions (and I cherry pick who I want to work with) so I know who offers great rates, great service, and fast funding options.

I also attend banking, credit, and fintech conferences, so I can keep a pulse on the ever-changing lending industry.

I've also been an entrepreneur for over 30 years. I've had online and offline businesses... everything from software development, retail shops, transportation businesses, and a whole lot in between. In that time, I've made a lot of money, and I've had my fair share of failures.

Having worked on both sides of the house, I know how extremely vital funding can be.

A lot of people (non-entrepreneurs, most of the time) think bootstrapping a business is some noble right-of-passage. That is, until you realize how hard it is to break out of the middle-class feast-or-famine cycle, when you're trying to penny pinch your way to success.

Don't let anybody lull you into thinking that you can start the next Facebook or Microsoft with $1,000 and a dream -- not every business is bootstrappable! Even if you want to open a little neighborhood corner store, you need capital! It ain't bootstrappable!

I have missed out on more than one multimillion dollar deal, because I didn't have the money to compete with software development teams that had a full-blown staff. I could put myself in the running and I could get the deals. But at that time, I didn't have the capital to pay for more people, so I lost out on a lot.

Even though I can't turn back the hands of time, I can help other entrepreneurs avoid all the missteps and mishaps that I encountered along the way. And a lot of that starts with understanding the entire self-funding universe.

What you'll be learning

I'm going to cover 3 key areas while you're here...

PART 1 discusses how lenders view you, the applicant. Some applications have automated approval, and in some cases, you'll need to talk to and meet with a lender. So, in this section you'll learn how to make the best impression from the very start, whether you're applying on or offline.

I'll talk about how lenders view your personal credit... your existing debt... and your financial background in general. Should you go through a manual review process, I'll tell you what an underwriter is looking at.

Then we'll talk about what lenders need to see when they give out preapprovals.

In PART 2, you'll see how lenders view your business. Here I'll show you six questions every business lender asks when you apply for a loan. I'll talk about collateral, including how lenders decide whether they'll accept it. You'll see how lenders view your industry in terms of risk. And this part is golden... you'll understand the best way to get funding based on your specific industry.

And in PART 3, you'll learn how documentation plays a role in the funding process. There are times when lenders will require a lot of documentation, and then there are situations when they'll ask for practically nothing. You'll be prepared in either case because I'm going to give you a list of items they're most likely to ask for, depending on the type of funding you're applying for.

This includes specific paperwork, your bank statements, your tax returns, and even financial statements. Plus, I'm going to detail exactly what they're looking for on each document. This will allow you to make course corrections just in case you need to make some quickie corrections.

The bottom line is, once you know what lenders are looking for, you can plan accordingly and get all the money you need, at any given time.

PART 1

How Lenders View YOU

A s I'm starting to do more speaking engagements, I'm meeting quite a few entrepreneurs with a similar story. They have bad personal credit, and they want to get business loans in their company name.

The general assumption is that your personal credit doesn't affect your ability to get business funding. Well, the 90's called, and they want their assumption back!

As much as I wish for the good old days when we had the decadent funding option of not crossing our personal credit profile with the business, that's not how it works anymore. Nowadays, the line between the two is blurred.

Your personal credit DOES matter in business funding. Not in all situations, but just enough that you can automatically assume it does. On top of that, business loans... I'm talking about 'cash-in-your-business-bank-account' loans... are usually one of the harder funding options to secure.

That's not to say that you can't get cash funding. You just need to understand what it's going to take to get that funding so you can plan accordingly.

Let me give you a couple of quick scenarios so you'll understand a little bit about the direction I'm going in.

Scenario #1

- ⊙ You're looking for a $30,000 business term loan.
- ⊙ You've been in business for at least 2 years.
- ⊙ Revenue is upwards of $150,000 a year.

You'll likely be able to get that loan in your company name. If everything else in your profile looks good, I'm thinking something along the lines of a low-interest SBA loan.

But there's a catch. The SBA lender is going to look at your personal credit. As a matter of fact, they're going to look at your personal credit score BEFORE they even look at your business credit. And if your personal credit score isn't up to snuff, the deal is dead before the paperwork even reaches your desk.

Scenario #2

- ⊙ You're looking for a $30,000 business term loan.
- ⊙ Your business is a startup (banks consider you a startup when your business is under two years old).
- ⊙ The business brings in upwards of $250,000 a year.

Well guess what, even if your business is making a pretty awesome $250,000 a year, a business lender offering a term loan is still going to look at your personal credit.

Kinda sounds like all small business owners have to be prepared to show their personal credit, doesn't it?

Well, you're right!

Small business owners (by default) are almost always subject to personal credit scrutiny.

And in many cases, your personal credit is just one aspect of the 'you' the banks are looking at.

Depending on the type of business loan, lenders may want to know about your experience and credentials in your field. They want to know what makes you qualified to run the business. The SBA pays very close attention to the 'who you are' part of your business plan, in addition to your personal credit.

That's why I wanted to talk about YOU, and how the YOU part plays into the funding process.

In this chapter we'll be looking at the many ways lenders view you, your credit, and your personal finances when they're making lending decisions.

Not every bank is going to look at every factor outlined here. Not every bank is going to weigh each factor in the same way. But most of what you see here will go into the decision-making process, even if it's an automated decision.

Think like a lender when looking at yourself

I was recently talking to a lender friend of mine.

He was telling me about a potential client -- we'll call her Claire. Claire is a small business owner who came to my friend seeking a $60,000 business loan.

He gave her a list of documents he would need to process the loan application. Within a few hours, she gave him everything except her financial statements.

My friend called her a few days later to inquire about the financial statements.

She said she was trying to get them from the accountant. Not a problem! Except, a couple weeks go by and it's the same story.

Now, don't get me wrong... it could have been a legitimate problem. Maybe something happened with her accountant. Maybe she found another lender. Or maybe Claire didn't have the financial statements, and she was trying to put them together. Who knows!

Either way, I could tell that my lender friend had already begun to form an opinion about her. And as you can imagine, it wasn't an extremely positive one.

Claire unknowingly violated one of the 5 C's of credit - *Character*. The 5 C's of credit is a simple smell test lenders use to gauge your creditworthiness, and to evaluate how much of a risk you pose as a borrower.

Oftentimes those 5 C's are baked into the bank's *underwriting guidelines*. Underwriting guidelines are the rules lenders formally establish for approving an applicant.

For example, a bank may require their business loan clients to be making at least $500,000 a year. They may require the owners of the business to have at least a 720 FICO 8 score. Each financial institution has their own underwriting guidelines based on how much of a risk they're willing to take.

Whatever parameters are in those underwriting guidelines becomes the basis of an automated approval or a denial. Or, if it's a small financial institution, you may be dealing with an individual who's manually screening you – similar to how my lender friend evaluated Claire on a 1-to-1 basis.

In the Character aspect of the 5 C's, a lender assesses who you are, as well as your financial character. They may look at your credit score, credit report, business reviews, social media profiles, etc.

A detailed look at the 5 C's

Here's what the 5 C's look like, and how they work in the lending process:

⊙ **Character** - When a lender views your credit report, credit scores and other publicly available information about you, they're making sure your financial profile matches their underwriting guidelines.

⊙ **Capacity** – This is your ability to pay a new debt. Lenders will look at your existing debts to determine if you have enough income/revenue to support additional debt. The calculation to determine this is the debt-to-income ratio (I cover the DTI ratio in this chapter, as well as Part 3.)

⊙ **Capital** - Your capital is basically your net worth. Do you have a home? Land? Vehicles? Cash in the bank? When it comes to small businesses, lenders want to know how liquid your assets are... in other words, how quickly can your goods be turned into cash if you were to hit a slow period?

⊙ **Collateral** - When a lender asks for collateral, they want to see what items can be sold off if you end up defaulting on a loan. For example, with equipment financing, the machinery you're purchasing is often used as collateral. If you fail to pay the loan, the equipment will be seized and sold off to pay as much of the loan as possible. (There's an entire section about collateral in Part 2.)

⊙ **Conditions** - Lenders will want to know the 'why' behind the loan. They'll also consider your industry... competitors... and the economy in general. These are things that can indirectly affect your ability to repay the loan.

Whenever I think of the 5 C's, I'm reminded of the old saying, *"You never get a second chance to make a first impression."*

In Claire's case, she didn't give the lender her financial statements when he asked for them. She didn't answer the phone when he called, nor did she return his phone calls.

Now suppose seven weeks later, Claire shows up with the financial statements. Sure, she has them, but the lender has already formed an opinion about the type of borrower she is. He's thinking, *"Hmmmm... will I have to chase Claire down for the loan payment every month?"*

And rightfully so! The lender certainly doesn't want to lose money on a borrower. If a small lender has too many defaulted loans, he has answer to his stakeholders.

And I can tell you that as a funding strategist, I value the relationship with my lending associates just as much as I value my small business clients. If I have to keep pounding the pavement for your paperwork, I'm not going to feel comfortable about handing your file over to a bank where I'm known and trusted for bringing in quality borrowers.

(This is actually one of the main reasons why I wrote this book. The money is out there, most people just don't know how to put their funding face on.)

I learned a long time ago that it's perfectly okay to turn clients away because of missteps just like this. Because when people show you who they are, believe them.

So, when thinking like a lender, be aware about how you present yourself and your business to the person whose making the decisions.

How to get an A+ in the character department

Character assessment begins with your credit profile and can progress in a multitude of directions. In fact, I want you to think of your credit profile as the door to the funding castle.

If your credit score is in the mid-700s and you've got a long credit history with no derogatory accounts, the door is going to be unlocked and you'll be able to walk right in. But if your score is in the low 600s, and you've got late payments and collection accounts, the door is going to be locked. A lender may need one key to open that door, or they may need several keys.

And that brings me to the first point for getting an A+ in the character department...

⊙ **Apply for funding before you need it, but also while your profile is strong enough to support it.** One of the biggest reasons why I'm so in favor of funding is because of a major business loss I experienced.

Back in 2007, I opened a high-end bike shop with my savings... more than $100,000. When the 2008 recession came around, the shop went under. People weren't buying titanium bikes. They were trying to figure out how not to lose their homes in the mortgage crash. That loss bled my bank account dry.

When I really sat down to think about all the mistakes I made, I immediately realized that had I funded that business, I would've still had my savings. I could have paid a bank loan and still had money to cover my everyday expenses.

But because I used all my money on the business and then lost it, I had no reserve. At that point, I couldn't even get funding for the business because of the economy. I'd been self-employed for 15 years at that point, and this was my first overwhelming failure.

That one mistake set me back a very long time both mentally and financially.

So, keep this in mind -- lenders love stability. They would rather lend to a business that's looking to grow, rather than one that appears to be in trouble. Therefore, the best time to get funding is when you don't look like you need it.

If you apply when your finances are on a downward spiral and you're clearly desperate for the money, you're going to have a harder (if not impossible) time getting what you need.

- ⊙ **Find lenders that match your profile.** I'm not knocking you if you have bad credit. I just want you to be realistic about what you can and cannot do with a shaky credit profile. That means you either find lenders who are going to be enthusiastic to work with you, or work with a funding strategist like me who can guide you. You don't want to waste your time trying to get in where you don't fit in.

- ⊙ **Have everything ready to go before you start the application process.** Number one... finish reading this book. I'm outlining everything AND the kitchen sink that you may need to get funding.

  Even if you're applying for a credit card, lenders will sometimes ask for specific paperwork. I want you to know what to have ready and why you need it. (The required document list is in Part 3.)

- ⊙ **Know your way around QuickBooks or have an accountant on your payroll.** Don't be like Claire, struggling and stressing about the numbers as she's knocking at the door!

  If you're applying for business funding (versus personal) you'll need to have access to financial statements. In fact, financial statements are sometimes necessary for getting insurance or even leasing certain pieces of equipment. (This is also covered in Part 3.)

Think like a lender when looking at your personal credit report

There are four credit reports lenders will choose from.

They come from the following credit bureaus (which you may also see referred to *as credit reporting agencies* or *CRAs*):

1. Experian
2. Equifax
3. Transunion
4. Innovis

You've probably heard about Experian, Equifax and Transunion, because those are also the bureaus where you can get a credit score.

But Innovis may have you thinking, *"What??? Who is that?"*

Innovis is actually the 4th largest credit bureau in the United States. They don't issue credit scores like the other three bureaus, but financial institutions often use Innovis as a secondary verification source.

So, if you're going to think like a lender, you'll need to get your hands on all four credit reports. And it's important that you get those credit reports directly from the credit bureaus themselves.

Where you get your credit report does matter

While you can certainly get your credit report from a website like Credit Karma, I don't recommend this.

For one thing, advertising-supported websites like Credit Karma may only carry your credit report from a single bureau. You'll need to see your reports from all the bureaus to ensure that everything is accurate across the board.

After all, if a lender is running your credit through Experian, and you've only looked at your Transunion credit report, you're at a disadvantage. You have no idea what's happening at Experian.

Secondly, if a credit report isn't obtained directly from the credit bureaus database, it may not include the same amount of data that you'd find on reports directly from the source. You want the exact same credit report that the banks are accessing, and nothing less.

This is why I specifically recommend getting your Experian, Equifax and Transunion credit reports from AnnualCreditReport.com. Or you can get your reports directly from the individual credit bureau websites. Neither of these options will cost you anything. (And remember, I have an entire webpage of all the links mentioned in this book at FundingPreppers.com/BookLinks.)

Since Innovis isn't offered at AnnualCreditReport.com, you must get that report directly from Innovis.com. That is the only place where you can get it.

What are lenders looking for in a credit report?

Remember, each lender has their own underwriting guidelines, which means what may get you approved at one bank, may not work at another.

The list below provides a general overview of what lenders are looking at. But if you want more precise underwriting guidelines, check out LocateYourLender.com.

LocateYourLender.com is an ever-growing directory of banks where you can source underwriting guidelines. These underwriting guidelines are not directly from the bank's mouth. Instead, it's a compilation of results and stats that Funding Prepper members have provided over the years.

With that said, let's put on our lender goggles and get to the basics.

⊙ **Do you have at least 3 tradelines with 18+ months of positive payment history?** A *tradeline* is a credit card, line of credit, or a loan account that appears on your credit report. Existing tradelines are important because lenders need to see how you handle debt.

For credit cards and lines of credit, lenders will look at the length of time those accounts have been open... limit for each account... your current balance... and payment history.

When it comes to loans, it's not a hardcore necessity for you to have one on your credit report. But when you do, it demonstrates an ongoing ability to pay down debt. And it doesn't matter if the loan account is open or closed and paid off. You may not always want to use your credit cards, but a loan shows consistent, positive payment history.

And that's the biggest takeaway here – on-time payment history is paramount. Not only do late payments severely damage your credit, depending on the lender, you may be outright denied funding.

So, what should you do if you don't have at least three tradelines with 18+ months of payment history?

Focus on paying your existing tradelines on time. It's better to have a single credit card with a $2,000 limit and no late payments, than a $20,000 card with two late payments.

⊙ **What's your current utilization rate?** Utilization is the amount of credit you use as compared to your total credit limit. In other words, it's your balance.

30% of your FICO 8 score (which I'll talk about in depth in the next section) is based on utilization. If your credit score has ever dropped like a rock after running up your credit cards during the holiday season, growing utilization (those high balances) is the reason why.

FICO calculates this portion of your score by looking at several things, including:

- **The number of accounts that have balances.** The more accounts with balances, the more points you lose.

- **The dollar amount you owe on all your accounts.** This isn't just how much you owe on your credit cards and lines of credit, but also installment loans like mortgages, car loans, student loans, and personal loans.

- **The percentage of individual credit card utilization.** If you have a $10,000 limit on a Visa, and you currently owe $9,000, I promise you, you're losing points. That's because you're using 90% of your credit limit, which is a known factor for point loss.

- **The percentage of aggregate utilization.** The utilization portion of your score considers how much you're using on individual credit cards. This is called *individual utilization.*

  Aggregate utilization is the total of your balances across all credit cards, as compared to the total credit limit. FICO recommends that you keep both individual and aggregate utilization below 30%.

  Therefore, if you had $50,000 in available credit across six credit cards, you would be losing big-time points if your aggregate utilization was at 62%.

  Even though point loss from utilization can be quite high, once you pay your credit cards off, you regain the points you lost.

This is why lenders will sometimes ask you to pay off a credit card before they'll approve you for a loan. If you have no other derogatory accounts on your credit report, lowering your utilization is an easy fix for raising your credit score.

- **The amount you owe on installment loans, as compared to the loan amount.** Owing $24,000 on a $25,000 loan is going to be viewed differently than if you only owe $3,200 on the same $25,000 loan.

  The lower amount of debt shows that you've been able to handle the payments, making you a good credit risk.

  This is not to say that you'll automatically be declined because you have existing debt. Lenders calculate your existing debt and compare it to your income to determine if you can handle more. I'll cover this in the debt-to-income sections.

⊙ **What is the age of your oldest tradeline?** The most ideal credit profile is an aged credit profile. And an aged credit profile is one where your oldest tradeline has been up and running for at least 36 months. Thirty-six months is a signal of stability, both to lenders and to how your credit score behaves.

For example, if Joanne's oldest tradeline is 12 months old, she may lose nine points after getting an inquiry on her credit report. However, Daniel may only lose two points if his oldest tradeline is 120 months.

In terms of strategy, this means you don't close the oldest account on your credit report while you're actively looking for funding -- especially if there are multiple years between your first and second oldest accounts.

Closing an account doesn't automatically knock it off your credit report. In fact, closed accounts may stay on your credit report for up to 10 years. And even if it's closed, it'll still show up as your oldest tradeline and affect your score accordingly.

But that's not a guarantee. I've seen closed accounts drop off the month after they were shuttered, causing a clients score to drop by as much as 23 points.

⊙ **How long has it been since a new tradeline was added to your credit report?** Lenders (especially business lenders) don't like to see a lot of recently added tradelines on your credit report.

For one thing, it introduces new inquiries to your credit. That's both a potential for point loss on your credit score, as well as a problem area for lenders who are inquiry-sensitive.

And it's not just the inquiry that can cause you to lose points.

If you got a new Visa in March, it would likely lower your credit score around April or May. As soon as that new account lands on your credit report, it lowers the *average age of accounts*, which is another metric lenders observe.

The average age of accounts is the average length of time that all your credit accounts have been open. It contributes to the *length of credit history* component of your credit score, which accounts for 15% of your total score.

A FICO High Achiever study revealed that people with 800+ FICO scores had an average age of credit accounts of 128 months -- which is a little over 10.5 years. Having a longer average age of accounts points to a more stable credit history. And as we know, lenders love stability.

Here's how you calculate the average age of accounts:

(Don't worry if you're a math-a-phobic, I've included a link to an average age of accounts calculator at *FundingPreppers.com/BookLinks*.)

1. Make a list of all your credit tradelines, including both open and closed accounts. If it's in your credit report, include it in the calculation.

2. For each account, calculate the age by determining the number of months that have passed since the account was opened.

3. Add up the account ages.

4. Now divide the number of accounts by the total age of all accounts. Voila! You've got the average age of accounts.

For example, let's say you have three accounts: 10 months, 20 months, and 30 months. Add those accounts.

10 + 20 + 30 = 60

Now divide the total age of all accounts, by the number of accounts.

60 / 3 accounts = 20 months

The average age of accounts in this example is 20 months.

The best way to tackle tradeline recency is to not get any new accounts at least 6 months before you apply for an important business loan. This is especially true if it's a sizable amount of money, say $100,000 or more.

If you need a loan, but you also have new tradelines on your credit report, then consider getting a personal loan or a line of credit. Consumer lenders tend to be more forgiving when it comes to having new tradelines.

Let *LocateYourLender.com* be your guide.

⊙ **Do you have any late payments?** If you don't have any late payments, congratulations. Do all you can to keep it that way.

Payment history – or how you pay your bills -- is 35% of your FICO score, which is the biggest piece of the credit score pie. This is the reason why just one late payment can single-handedly lower your credit score 30-60+ points.

The worst I've ever seen was an insane 101-point drop. I'm pretty sure my client cried when she saw that one staring her in the face. It certainly broke my heart, and it wasn't even mine!

If you do have lates, lenders will look at several things including:

⊙ The number of late payments you have,

⊙ When they occurred (recent lates are viewed more harshly than those from 2-6 years ago),

⊙ If they all occurred consecutively or during separate time periods,

⊙ If the late(s) are on a single account or multiple accounts.

Regardless of how old a late payment is, it can still be cause for denial.

Fortunately, the older a late gets, the less it tends to affect your credit score. And once it passes the two-year mark, you'll slowly begin regaining points you lost.

Just know you'll never gain all those points back until the late payment drops off at the seven-year mark. If you have multiple late payments, you'll have to wait till the final one is gone before your score fully stabilizes.

As you can see, late payments can have a tremendous chokehold over your credit score. And waiting for them to drop off may feel like torture when you're ready to move upward and onward.

So, if you don't feel like patiently waiting for nature to take it's course, the alternative would be to send a *goodwill letter* to the creditor.

A goodwill letter is simply a request. You're asking the creditor to permanently delete the late payment(s) from your credit report. In the credit industry, this is known as a *goodwill adjustment*, and yes... it's perfectly legal.

Even still, credit card companies can be beastly, and dealing with overseas customer service reps can drive you bananas. But as I tell my clients, don't let the logistics of this situation make a fool out of you.

If you screwed up, humble yourself and let the letter writing begin – (which in reality, may end up being multiple letters).

The consensus is that one letter *(or email)* may not do the trick. You may need to blast out a letter/email to the customer service department once a month. In some cases, clients have had good results contacting the CEO of the company, as well as customer service. (Yup, at the same time.)

Sometimes it really does work, and you get those lates removed. When that happens, your points are regained as if nothing happened.

Sometimes you must continue this routine for multiple months before you see results.

And then there will be times when you won't have any luck with this technique. Maybe the creditor outright tells you that they're not going to respond to your requests.

Some creditors absolutely will not provide goodwill adjustments. Bank of America is a no-go, and they make that perfectly clear on their website. Chase has also publicly stated that they're not doing them.

Outside of those two, if you have a good payment history before and after the late(s) then a goodwill letter makes sense. If you've had at least 3-6 months of positive payment history since your late payment(s), even better. It shows that the late payment was an isolated incident. That's exactly how you'll explain it in the letter.

Recent lates are most damaging to your credit, but even if you can get older lates removed, that's great too. Any late payment that you get removed is going to help your credit score. Remember, we're talking about 35% of your score here, so IT IS a big deal.

FYI: You'll find a goodwill letter template at (FundingPreppers.com/BookLinks).

⊙ **Do you have any charge-offs?** If late payments are a big deal, charge-offs are what I consider the gold medal winner of the bad credit Olympics. And you do not want to be on the podium to receive this award!

When you don't make a payment on an outstanding credit card or loan, it can get charged off 120-180 days after your last payment. At that point, the lender has written the loan off as uncollectable.

The charged-off account can either be sold to a debt buyer (for pennies on the dollar), or the creditor will hold on to the debt and possibly sue you. Either way, the derogatory account now stays on your credit report for seven years after your last payment.

So, where's the win-win in any of this?

The real win happens if you pay off the old debt before it gets sold to a debt buyer or sent to a collection agency. Once that debt is sold, you end up with a charge-off AND a collection account on your credit report. That's two derogatory accounts for the price of one.

Bad credit is one thing. But bad credit that goes unpaid while you're also seeking more funding typically doesn't get you any extra credit points in the character department.

You may not be able to get prime lending options with paid charge-offs, but you will be able to find some decent lenders who are willing to work with you if the charge-off is over two years old and your income is decent.

⊙ **Do you have any collection accounts?** As I previously mentioned, a collection account will show up on your credit report after a tradeline has been charged off, or if you have an unpaid hospital bill.

Like any other derogatory account, it will lower your credit score. And yes, collection accounts can be a deal breaker for many forms of funding, including credit cards.

You may only have a chance with certain lenders if the collection account has been paid off... is over 5 years old, or if it's a hospital bill. This is the kind of stuff covered over at LocateYourLender.com.

⊙ **Do you have a foreclosure on your credit report?** Foreclosures can be harsh. Even Experian says, *"Lenders view a foreclosure as a serious negative event in your credit history, second in severity only to bankruptcy."* It's obviously one of the more difficult credit scenarios to work around.

And if the foreclosure is an FHA loan with an outstanding debt, it'll show up in the CAIVRS database, which means you won't be able to get an SBA loan. (I'll talk about the CAIVRS database a little later.)

Even if it's not an FHA loan, if it's less than five years old, it may still be considered too new of a debt in lender's eyes. More so than focusing on trying to score big money funding deals right now, I would work on rebuilding your credit so that you're ready to roll when things get better.

⊙ **Do you have a bankruptcy on your credit report?** The unfortunate truth is that a personal bankruptcy can cause an immediate "No!" from most lenders, even when it comes to business loans.

Can you get funding? Yes, but you're limited to what you'll be approved for. Some lenders will only work with you if the bankruptcy is over a certain age, like 6 months old or 2 years old.

If you're a subscriber to LocateYourLender.com, you can search for banks that provide funding if you have a bankruptcy. I've also listed important details about how old that bankruptcy needs to be before you can apply for funding with a specific lender.

Think like a lender when looking at your credit score

Borrowers tend to think that a credit score shows how well you've been paying your bills.

But when you think like a lender, you'll know that your credit score shows how much of a risk you are.

Lenders call this risk d*efault probability*. It reflects the likelihood that a borrower won't repay a debt. The lower your credit score, the higher the default probability.

30

According to a FICO study, if your credit score is between 750-850, you only have a 1% chance of defaulting on a credit card or loan. Those in the 700-749 range have a 4.4% chance of default. With a 650-699, you have a probability default rate of 8.9%. Between 550-559, that number goes up to 22.5%. And if you're below 549, your default probability ranges from 28.4%-41%.

Based on that alone, the goal is to always keep your credit score over the 750 range. (And really, I believe 760 is an even sweeter spot.)

An overview of the FICO Score universe

There are 28 different FICO scores. Besides the general FICO 8, 9 and 10 scores, there are also mortgage scores, scores for car loans, and credit card scores. (Scores galore!)

Each score is built from the same five factors.

- ⊙ **Payment History:** 298 points -- 35%
- ⊙ **Utilization (Amount Owed):** 255 points -- 30%
- ⊙ **Length of Credit History:** 128 points – 15%
- ⊙ **Credit Mix:** 85 points – 10%
- ⊙ **New Credit:** 85 points – 10%

Actions taken within those factors are weighed differently depending on the score.

For example, mortgage scores put more weight on inquiries and the amount of new credit you've gotten.

This is why mortgage brokers recommend that you don't open any new accounts two years before you want to buy a house. New accounts lower your mortgage scores significantly more than other scores.

Furthermore, since each bureau uses their own algorithm, a new account may take more points from your Experian mortgage score, than Transunion or Equifax.

The most widely used FICO credit score

Most (not all) financial institutions base their decisions on the FICO 8 score.

Some lenders use the Experian FICO 8... some will use Equifax FICO 8... and others will choose the Transunion FICO 8. There are three different versions of FICO 8 because each bureau calculates it differently.

Business lenders (loans) tend to look at your FICO 8's at all three bureaus.

Consumer lenders (loans and credit cards) usually only check your FICO 8 score through a single bureau. For instance, American Express uses Experian FICO 8 to make lending decisions.

And then you have certain outliers -- like Capital One – that will run your FICO 8 scores through all three credit bureaus. It is for this reason alone that I won't apply for a Capital One card. I refuse to take an inquiry hit at all three bureaus for a bank that's well-known for keeping people at certain credit limits.

(Remember I said earlier that Capital One takes on riskier borrowers? Well, this is the cost you pay when you're a risky borrower.)

Where to get your FICO credit scores

I recommend you get all 28 of your FICO scores directly from the source – MyFICO.com.

This company isn't just a reseller of FICO scores. MyFICO is where FICO scores were born. The legendary FICO algorithm was cooked up here in 1989.

My second choice for obtaining FICO scores is www.Experian.com.

I love Experian.com because they update the Experian FICO scores every single day. This is exclusive just to Experian. (MyFICO provides updates once a month, at most.)

Experian.com is perfect for Funding Preppers because you can track how your score goes up or down, depending on the moves you make. This may not seem like such a big deal now.

But when you understand how many points you lose from paying the minimum balances on your credit cards... or how many you gain when you completely pay your debts off, you begin to understand what you'll need to do to create an optimal credit score.

I've been monitoring my credit scores on Experian.com for 3+ years. Every month I detail my balances, new inquiries, as well as funding obtained. And then I document all of this, including how my scores have evolved over time, in my Fearlessly Seeking Funding newsletter (FearlesslySeekingFunding.com).

The only downside to Experian.com is that they don't do daily updates for Equifax or Transunion scores. However, they do provide Equifax and Transunion FICO 8 scores on a monthly basis, with the $25 a month membership.

Where NOT to get your FICO credit scores

If you're not going to use MyFICO or Experian.com, understand that Credit Karma and MyWallet.com do not provide FICO scores. The Equifax and Transunion websites also do not provide FICO scores.

All these sites offer the VantageScore only.

VantageScore is a consumer credit scoring model created by Experian, Equifax and Transunion in 2006. Unlike FICO, that has separate scores for each bureau, VantageScore has a single tri-bureau score.

Despite the fact that VantageScore is the model used on almost all 'free credit score' websites, it is not the credit score that most lenders use. That may change in the future. But for now, FICO is first.

Also, there may be times when your FICO 8 and your VantageScore look similar. But I can assure you, that's purely by coincidence. These two scoring models each have their own algorithm, which means they're calculated differently. A factor that weighs one way on VantageScore, may weigh differently on FICO.

Take medical collection accounts, for example.

The VantageScore 3 model ignores both paid and unpaid medical collections. The FICO 8 model only ignores medical collections that are under $100, or less than 365 days old.

Therefore, a two-year old, $1,500 medical collection won't influence VantageScore 3, but it will cause a drop on FICO 8.

How does your score fit in the funding fold?

Now that you've had a chance to get your FICO 8's all lined up, let's see how your scores fare in the funding world.

760-850

Congrats, FICO baller! You're at the peak of the credit score game. Anytime your score is past 760, you should have no problem being approved for loans or credit cards, provided you meet the lender's other requirements. This is also where you tend to qualify for the lowest interest rates and the best repayment terms.

However, as advantageous as a 760+ looks, there are also a few things you need to keep in mind.

If your score is built on a foundation of retail store cards, sub-prime credit cards (like Credit One), or if you're an authorized user on several cards, you're basically living in a credit house made of straw.

Having a great score is key to getting funded. But lenders also look at what creates that great score.

For example, when my daughter was 17, I put her on several of my credit cards as an authorized user. By the time she turned 18, her FICO 8's were around 740's to 760ish.

She was immediately approved for her first credit card, with a starting limit of $1,200.

This is a low amount, considering her scores were in peak condition. However, you must consider that her initial score was built solely on her status as an authorized user. She also had very low income.

The moral of the story is that a high credit score will get you approved... but your overall credit profile ultimately decides your funding limit fate.

If you've got a 762 FICO 8, and your credit report shows $70,000 in available credit, spread across 3 credit cards, with only a $500 balance, and $81,000 in yearly income, then your funding limits are going to be much higher than my 18-year-old in the same score range, with authorized user status and $11,000 in income.

740-759

You're close to peak condition and likely won't have a problem being approved at most financial institutions, on either the business or personal side.

720-739

You'll be approved for most loans, credit cards and lines of credit, but this range is like being at the cusp. Your score can go much higher, if you play the sit-and-wait game. Or it can drop below 700 really fast with enough funding plays and increased utilization.

Be sure you're making very deliberate funding moves. Look for preapproval applications, so you're not wasting inquiries. Ask for credit limit increases on cards where no hard inquiry is required.

If you're planning to get a few new credit cards in this zone, be prepared to take an application rest for 6+ months to give your scores a chance to recover.

700-719

Being over 700 is great and you will be approved for many forms of funding. Just don't get too comfortable. This is still a range where denials exist -- especially if you're dealing with lenders who have high standards.

This is also where preapprovals make the most sense. See what you're being offered in the mail or online at LocateYourLender.com. Just keep in mind that depending on the depth and strength of your credit profile, you may see lower limit cards here.

This is the time where I'll work to solidify my relationships with existing lenders. I'll pay down my balances. I'll double and triple my loan payments. Funding Preppers know when it's time to party and when it's time to plant seeds.

670-699

Although these aren't terrible scores by themselves, in terms of getting funded, I consider this the danger zone.

Approvals may be hit-or-miss in this range. Interest rates will likely be at the high end. Funding is do-able here, but you'll need to have realistic expectations about what you can get and who you can get it from. Your choice of lenders is going to be limited.

669 and below

I know this isn't the most pleasant place to be. And I won't sugarcoat it... In terms of funding, you won't get a lot of great offers that are based on your credit score. When you do get offers, expect higher interest rates. Expect terms that may make you go, "Uuuuuuugh!" In some cases, you'll need to show more documentation and paperwork than if you came in with higher scores.

The upside is that you may be able to get funded based on factors outside of your credit score. You can have bad credit, and still get funded based on your income. You may be able to get funded on your outstanding invoices.

Although they're not as popular as credit cards and cash loans, there are a handful of funding options that allow you to have shaky credit. And don't worry... I'll be covering those options in Part 4.

The un-sneaky way I used this knowledge to get $90,000+ in credit within a year

Now that you understand that most banks are only going to look at a single credit bureau to make an approval decision, and you know what your FICO 8 scores look like, you can start using this knowledge to your advantage.

The strategy you're about to learn is how I managed to rake up more than $90,000 in credit cards -- during the height of the COVID pandemic. This was probably one of the worst times to apply for credit cards, since banks were notoriously giving out lower-than-usual limits. And yet, I still managed to beautifully grow my credit profile.

This strategy was the main reason why I created the LocateYourLender.com directory back in 2020. At the time, I was providing Credit Audits to clients with bad credit.

If you know anything about credit repair, then you know that half of the process is about getting rid of the negative stuff, and the other half is about adding positive accounts to aid in rebuilding and increasing your credit score.

In that regard, Locate Your Lender became a source to help my Credit Audit clients find lenders where they could potentially rebuild.

Over the years, we've been adding financial institutions for all credit score levels. But this isn't just a list of banks... these are guidelines. Lots and lots of guidelines. While I certainly can't guarantee you'll be approved for everything, the guidelines are detailed enough that you'll know where you have the greatest chances for approvals.

One last thing... I still want you to read the rest of the book before you jump right into this strategy. It's vital that you have a full understanding of how the funding process works before you decide which direction you'd like to go. This is just one path. You may decide that you'd like to tackle things in a different way.

1. **First, you'll need access to your FICO 8 credit scores.**
2. **Make note of your highest score.** This is the bureau you'll be working with first.
3. **If your utilization is above 20%, pay down some of your debt as close as you can get to below 9%, to increase your scores.** This is optional, but I recommend you go in with the best score possible. Try to be above 760 so you'll know what your profile is capable of at its very best.
4. **Go to LocateYourLender.com and make a list of banks that run your credit through the bureau with your highest FICO 8 score.** In other words, if your Experian FICO 8 is the highest of the three, then you'll be looking for banks that use Experian FICO 8 for approvals. Make sure you're choosing

banks that align with your entire credit profile, in addition to your high FICO score.

5. **Repeat step #4 for your second and third highest FICO 8 scores.**

6. **From your three lists, choose one bank for each bureau.** These should be the banks where you're almost 100% sure that you'll be approved. If your credit is kinda shaky, then look for preapprovals and Revealers on Locate Your Lender. (Revealers are banks that tell you how much you've been approved for before you get the hard inquiry.)

7. **Apply to all three banks on the same day.** This way, when the accounts hit your credit report, they all hit at once. Yes, this is going to lower your credit scores across all three bureaus. However, as the new accounts age together, you'll regain those points collectively.

Think like a lender when investigating "hidden data" about you

Besides your credit reports, lenders (especially business lenders) may also review your financial background using alternative sources.

They may go to specialty databases like:

Tax Guard - Where they'll find out if you have outstanding debt, missing tax returns, or federal tax liens.

Cogency Global - Where lenders can find out if you have a UCC filing against your business. The UCC filing will tell them whether you have another business loan that you're not disclosing.

Public Access to Court Electronic Records (PACER) - Lenders can find out if you've filed for bankruptcy through PACER, even if the bankruptcy isn't on your credit report.

Or they'll go directly to consumer reports. (Nope, not the *Consumer Reports* magazine, that you probably know nothing about unless you're over the age of 46.)

A consumer report is a document containing information compiled from a variety of public and private databases. They're like the private databases I just mentioned, as they contain information not found in your credit report.

For example, judgements are no longer placed on credit reports (as of April 2018), but they can still be found in certain databases and consumer reports. And that's because judgements are publicly available in courthouse records.

One of the most incredible consumer reports I've ever seen comes from LexisNexis. They have a product called a Consumer Disclosure Report that will blow your friggin' mind.

This Report contains information like:

- Addresses where you've lived,
- Phone numbers attached to your name,
- Post-secondary educational records,
- Relationships between you and family members (I wish I was joking),
- Real estate you own and have owned,
- Tax assessment records for property you own,
- Home and auto insurance records,
- Professional licenses you have (pilots license, for example),
- Businesses you've owned, or where your name was on the registration,
- Debts you owe (like child support),
- Vehicles registered in your name,

- ⊙ Moving violations, accident claims and other motor vehicle records,

- ⊙ Judgements and liens against you,

- ⊙ Bankruptcy records,

- ⊙ And quite possibly much more than that, depending on how colorful your life has been.

Law enforcement people use the Consumer Disclosure Report.

Attorneys use it.

Certain debt collectors use it.

And yes, lenders will use it for very specific situations.

And they utilize it because a consumer report is like the ultimate tattletale, who doesn't forget any of the bad stuff you do.

Unlike credit reports, which only have 7.5 years' worth of derogatory accounts (unless it's a Chapter 7 bankruptcy, which stays on your credit for 10 years), there are no time limitations for removing derogatory information from a consumer report. If you got a lien 15 years ago, that lien is likely still in a consumer report, even if you paid it off.

This doesn't mean every bad thing automatically gets counted against you. I personally have several judgments on my Consumer Disclosure Report, and my ability to get funding has not been hindered.

Like I said, lenders will only use it for certain situations. In general, they're not going to pull out the heavy-duty guns of a Consumer Disclosure Report for a $20,000 loan. However, they probably are going to be a bit more Sherlock Holmesy for $250,000.

Either way, I like to let Funding Preppers know what's out there so you're aware of how deep the investigative rabbit hole can go. It's a nod to being honest with your application actions, because databases will snitch on you faster and more efficiently than you can imagine.

So now that you know this, how do you think like a lender moving forward?

Well, you'll definitely need a copy of the most widely used consumer reports to make sure that everything listed is 100% accurate. This is VERY important, as these reports are known to have errors.

In fact, look at what's stated in the LexisNexis Accurint terms of service:

> *"Due to the nature of public record information, the public records and commercially available data sources used in the LN Services may contain errors. Source data is sometimes reported or entered inaccurately, processed poorly or incorrectly, and is generally not free from defect.*
>
> *LN Services are not the source of data, nor are they a comprehensive compilation of the data."*

And this type of disclaimer isn't exclusive to just LexisNexis. Anytime you have a database of compiled information, there's a possibility of error. What's interesting is how those errors can affect you, even if a lender doesn't use the actual consumer report.

Inaccurate data = More inaccurate data

I once had a client who always got the security verification questions wrong whenever she tried to order her credit reports from AnnualCreditReport.com. When she came to me, she was a nervous wreck thinking that someone had stolen her identity. Turns out it was a glitch in the consumer report matrix.

Those verification questions are usually pulled from data in your LexisNexis Consumer Disclosure Report. And if any of that data is incorrect or inaccurate, you're probably going to get those security questions wrong.

Unfortunately, once your data is inaccurate in one database, that same inaccurate information may trickle down to other databases.

This is why it's so important to get these reports, and to dispute any incorrect information before you apply for funding.

Which "hidden data" sources are lenders using?

Below you'll find a list of consumer reports lenders may use. You can get a copy of each one every 12 months. (I have an alarm set in my Google calendar alerting me for when it's time to request an update. You don't have to get ready if you stay ready!)

As always, links for these reports can be found at (FundingPreppers.com/BookLinks).

Start with the LexisNexis Consumer Portal, where you'll be able to order the Consumer Disclosure Report. They're going to ask you for some personal information, including your social security number, so don't be alarmed.

Then you'll grab your Accurint Comprehensive Report, which LexisNexis also distributes. Accurint is used by banking professionals to facilitate collections, asset identification, foreclosures, and fraud. If you find any mistakes on the LexisNexis Consumer Disclosure Report, it's likely that you'll also find them here on the Accurint Comprehensive Report.

Next, get your CoreLogic Credco Consumer Report. Lenders (particularly mortgage and auto lenders) use Credco for their tri-merge credit report, which is a merged combination of your Experian, Equifax and Transunion credit reports. Keep in mind, if you have any errors on those three credit reports, they're also going to show up on the Credco report.

According to the Consumer Financial Protection Bureau (CFPB), your CoreLogic Credco Consumer Report may also have compiled information about property ownership and home loan obligation records; property legal filings and tax payment status; rental applications and collection accounts; consumer bankruptcies, liens, judgments, and child support obligations.

Last, get a copy of your ChexSystems report. If you're thinking about going through a credit union for a credit card or a personal loan, you'll need to open a new account with that credit union – and that's where ChexSystems comes into play. Most credit unions run your information through ChexSystems before they allow you to open a checking or savings account.

ChexSystems contains information about bank accounts you've overdrawn, checks you've bounced, and other transactions flagged as fraudulent on your bank accounts within the past 5 years. If you've never done any of the above, then your ChexSystems report will be clear, except for any accounts you've opened.

Think like a lender when examining your debt

Besides derogatory accounts, the amount of debt you're carrying is one of the biggest reasons why you'll be denied funding. And to double down on that, if you're applying for a business loan, lenders will look at both your personal and your business' debt.

It all goes back to those 5 C's of credit I spoke about earlier.

When it comes to your debt, we're talking about your *Capacity* to repay a new loan. Lenders will want to know if you can afford to take on additional debt, and they'll be looking for certain red flags in your credit profile that point to financial struggle.

So, if you're going to think like a lender, let's clean up any potential debt deficiencies before you start submitting those applications.

Do you have a high debt-to-income (DTI) ratio?

In the lending business, the DTI ratio is one of the most widely used measurements for risk assessment. It's also one of the main factors that determines your funding limits. The lower your DTI, the more likely you are to be approved and given higher limits.

1. **To calculate this powerful percentage, you'll first add all the DTI-friendly bills you pay monthly.** This could include your mortgage/rent, timeshare payments, car loans, personal loans, student loans, minimum payments on credit cards and child support.

   Rent/Mortgage - $1,200

   Credit card bills - $200

   Car loans - $477

   TOTAL MONTHLY DEBT = $1,877

2. **Now list your gross monthly income (before taxes).**

   GROSS MONTHLY INCOME = $7,110

3. **Divide your monthly debt by gross monthly income.**

   1,877 / 7,110 = 0.263

4. **Turn that total into a percentage and say hello to your DTI ratio.**

   DTI RATIO = 26%

Where do you spy your DTI?

Under 35%? This is the sweet spot lenders like to see! It shows that you still have cash leftover after paying your monthly bills, and you won't have issues taking on additional debt

36%-43%? Depending on the type of funding you're seeking, it's touch-and-go here. If you have an existing relationship with a lender, or you have a long, positive credit history, you may be granted some leniency. But once you're in that 40% range, it gets harder to receive limits that make a difference.

Over 44%? Don't do it. You don't want to apply for anything while you're here because it signals financial struggle.

Do you have high credit card utilization?

We spoke about credit card utilization a little earlier in this chapter. It's the amount of debt you owe, divided by your credit limit. Your FICO 8 score is based on the utilization of individual credit cards, as well as the total utilization of all your credit cards.

FICO says you should keep your total utilization below 30%. I agree with that part. I've let my utilization get as high as 62% and the point loss is brutal. Even without any derogatory accounts, my FICO 8 fell below 660. And just to give you some reference, I was hovering around 760 when my utilization was below 10%.

So yes, 30% utilization is a respectable goal. But for the sake of keeping your credit profile funding-ready, your utilization should ideally be below 6%. And if you truly want to see the biggest bang for your application buck, keep it in the 1%-2% range.

Will you be able to get funding if you're over 6% utilization? Of course, you will! If you're a FearlesslySeekingFunding.com subscriber, then you already know I've gotten well-funded with 15%-20% utilization.

Just keep in mind that the higher your utilization, the less amount of money you stand to be approved for.

And if your credit cards are maxed out, or close to being maxed out, that's like a big red stop sign for lenders. It's not even worth wasting your time with an application.

Now let's look at how to calculate total utilization.

1. **First add your total credit limit across all credit cards.**

   Chase Visa - $5,000 limit

   Bank of America Visa - $15,500 limit

   Amazon store card - $3,000 limit

   Discover - $7,000 limit

   TOTAL CREDIT LIMIT = $30,500

2. **Add the total amount you owe on each credit card.**

   Chase Visa - $5,000 limit / $87 balance

   Bank of America Visa - $15,500 limit / $1,326 balance

   Amazon store card - $3,000 limit / $0 balance

   Discover - $7,000 limit / $5,209 balance

   TOTAL AMOUNT OWED (UTILIZATION) = $6,622

3. **Divide the amount owed by the total credit limit.**

   6,622 / 30,500 = 0.217

4. **Turn that decimal into a percentage.**

   TOTAL UTILIZATION = 22%

How high is too high when it comes to utilization?

1%-2% Utilization: This is where you'll see the greatest number of approvals and the highest limits. If your FICO 8 is in a good place, and you haven't applied for new credit in the past 12+ months, you should be pleasantly surprised by your limits.

3%-5% Utilization: Life is great! But if you're teetering close to a 760 FICO 8 score, pay your debts down below 3% to get the extra points before applying for funding. It's kind of one of those no-brainer ways to make sure you're in the best position possible

6%-9% Utilization: You're still safe. You may notice slightly more point loss than the previous two thresholds.

10%-18% Utilization: Heavier point loss typically occurs after you cross the 10% mark. You're safe. But this might be where you'll need to curb your enthusiasm as far as limits you can expect when applying.

19%-28% Utilization: Alrighty... the fire has officially started touching your toes. I don't suggest you apply for any personal loans once your utilization tops 25%.

29%+ Utilization: The reality of the situation is that you will be able to get funding from someone, somewhere. But is it worth it? Nah. And if you're reading this during some funky economic period, then I'm gonna give it a hard nahhhhh.

Your goal isn't to just get funding. It's to get the most that you possibly can whenever you apply. Having 36% utilization, or 44%, or 50% isn't how you achieve that goal.

Do you have unpaid derogatory debt?

We talked about derogatory accounts a little earlier. These are bankruptcies, foreclosures, repossessions, charge-offs, collection accounts, and any debts that haven't been paid off within the past seven years.

The problem with not paying off old debt is that it shows you're not willing to pay your bills. In terms of the 5 C's of credit, you're showing poor Character and Capacity.

Do you have federal loans you defaulted on?

CAIVRS (Credit Alert Interactive Verification Reporting System) is a database containing information about people who have defaulted on federal loans.

If you haven't paid your federal student loans, you're in there. If you haven't paid back an SBA loan, you're in there. If your FHA-backed mortgage was foreclosed on and the government had to pay the bank, yup... you're in CAIVRS.

The following agencies report unpaid loans, foreclosures and liens to this database:

- Department of Housing and Urban Development (HUD)
- Department of Education (DOE)
- Department of Veterans Affairs (VA)
- Department of Agriculture (USDA)
- Small Business Administration (SBA)
- Department of Justice (DOJ)

The general public isn't allowed to access the CAIVRS database. But if you apply for an SBA loan, the lender will run your social security number and your EIN to see if you're there. If you show up in CAIVRS, it's an instant denial, no matter how good your credit is.

Keep in mind, only federal agencies use CAIVRS. If you're not getting an SBA loan, a private lender wouldn't know that you've defaulted on a federal loan unless it appears on your credit, or it's discovered in a consumer report.

Do you have deferred debt?

By deferred debt, I mean student loans that are currently in deferment. Most lenders don't include deferred student loans in DTI calculations; however, some do.

Even though it's outside the scope of this book, if you're trying to obtain a conventional mortgage, deferred student loans are included in the DTI ratio at either .05% or 1% of the balance.

Just to be on the safe side, I recommend you include .05% of your deferred student loans in your DTI ratio calculations. This way if a bank includes it, you've already factored it in.

Think like a lender so you can get credit card and loan preapprovals

I call preapprovals the low hanging fruit of funding opportunities.

They may not land in your mailbox every day, but when they do, they can be good for $2,000-$40,000+ in funding.

Unfortunately, there's no way to guarantee that you'll receive preapprovals. But if you understand how they land in your mailbox, you may be able to increase your chances of receiving them.

It all starts with the Fair Credit Reporting Act (FCRA). The FCRA allows banks, credit unions and other financial institutions to obtain lists of consumers that meet a pre-defined criterion. They obtain these lists from Experian, Equifax and Transunion. Provided you have not opted-out to receive preapprovals, and you meet the bank's specific criteria, you may eventually receive them.

Here's how the process works...

1) **First, a bank creates a list of criteria for customers they want to offer the preapproval to.** Some of the criteria might include:

- Credit score that is above or below a certain threshold,
- Minimum income level,
- Existence of a credit card,
- Existence of a credit card with a certain limit,
- Existence of a paid off loan,
- No loans on the credit report,

- Distance from the bank branch,

- Presence of a late payment,

- No derogatory accounts on the credit report.

For example, ABC Bank may request 10,000 names that match a request like this:

- FICO 8 credit score above 700,

- No derogatory marks on the credit report,

- Personal income above $50,000,

- No more than 5 miles from a bank branch.

2) **The bank gives that list to the credit bureau, and the credit bureau sends the bank a list of consumers who match what they're looking for.**

The credit bureau can only send the bank the consumer's name and address. They cannot include information that ties you to a specific lender, creditor or financial institution.

A prescreening bank doesn't know who you have other accounts with. This is why it's possible to get accounts with prime lenders, even if you've only had accounts with sub-prime lenders.

3) **When the bank receives the list of consumers from the credit bureau, the bank is required to make a *firm offer of credit* to consumers who receive their mailer.**

This means if you receive a preapproval letter and you apply for funding, the bank must honor that firm offer of credit *as long as you have continued to meet the prescreened criteria and you have the necessary collateral, which should be mentioned in the offer.*

That's the important part! It could take 2-3 months from the time the bank receives your info, until the time you apply.

You could receive a preapproval in May, but if your credit score has gone from a 768 in March to a 644 in May, that preapproval may not be honored anymore.

Also, when you apply, you can still be denied based on information you submit on the application. The bank cannot deny you based on your credit, if your credit report is still the same. But they can deny you based on income or other information included on the credit application.

It may look like a preapproval, but it's not

In an effort to get you to apply, banks will sometimes send mailers that look and sound like preapprovals. It's important to pay attention to these imposters, so that you don't end up applying for funding that you're not qualified for. (This is one of the swiftest ways to get a denial!)

Here are some simple tell-tale signs to determine if your mailer is a preapproval or a marketing piece:

⊙ **If there's a single APR for Purchases, it's usually a preapproval. However, when there's a range of APR's for Purchases, it's a marketing mailer.**

Every mailer will include a list of Terms and Conditions for the product they want you to apply for. Usually, the first item on the list is the Annual Percentage Rate (APR for Purchases). If there's one percentage listed in that column, like 6.2%, then it's probably a preapproval. But if there's a range of percentages, like 9%-22.5%, it's always a marketing mailer.

⊙ **A preapproval will explicitly say *preapproved*.** Banks cannot use the term preapproved unless they're making a firm offer of credit to the recipient.

⊙ If it says *pre-selected or pre-qualified*, it is NOT a definite **pre-approval.** This is typical marketing verbiage. Don't be fooled!

⊙ If it says, *you've been selected to apply for...*, it's not a **preapproval.** Again, typical marketing-speak.

I'm not saying that you shouldn't apply to these banks. I'm just giving you a heads up that if you're looking for a preapproval you have to be aware of what a real preapproval looks like.

PART 2

How Lenders View Your BUSINESS

Regardless of whether you're applying for business credit or a business loan, your company is always going to be put under the lender's microscope.

This section will help you understand:

- How the type of business you're running affects the funding options that are available to you,

- Whether it's best to pay yourself a salary or not,

- What types of collateral lenders are looking for?

- How to get access to your business credit scores,

- How to build your business credit profile so that you'll get high-limit business credit cards and loans.

But before we get knee deep into this conversation, let's look at when it makes sense to get funding in your company name and when it's best to rely on consumer funding (loans and credit in your personal name).

I want you to wrap your head around this part early in the decision-making process so that as you're reading, you have a better understanding of which direction you'd like to go in.

Personal loans vs. Business loans

Applying for a business loan is going to require more paperwork and question answering than applying for a personal loan.

If you just need a quick $10,000-$30,000, your FICO 8 scores are above 720, and you intend on paying the loan back in full within 3-24 months - a personal loan might be faster and easier to get than a business loan.

This is especially true if you need startup money, since business lenders won't work with you unless the business is generating revenue. Startups usually have no choice except for a personal loan or business credit cards.

The downside of getting a personal loan is that it shows up on your personal credit. A personal loan will add to your debt-to-income ratio. This could affect your ability to get additional loans for other life expenses - (like a mortgage). Also, since a personal loan adds a new tradeline to your credit report, it lowers your credit score.

Obviously if you pay a personal loan off quick enough, you don't have to worry about any of these issues. And once a loan is paid off, it no longer counts towards your debt-to-income ratio. In addition, a paid off loan on your personal credit is a bonus. It shows other lenders that you are trustworthy enough to handle long-term debt.

Business loans, on the other hand, typically require more documentation than personal loans. This is true even at the $10,000-$20,000 level.

To get a business loan, your business must be making a certain amount of money each month. And you'll almost always need to show 3-12 months' worth of business bank statements to prove that cashflow. If your bank statements show you're making under $10,000 a month, it's going to be difficult to get a business loan over $10,000.

Many business lenders also require 2-3 years' worth of tax returns, including all related schedules. And if that's not enough, you'll still need to have good personal credit, even if it's a business loan.

And that's just the basics, because an SBA loan requires even more documentation than that. (Though keep in mind, SBA loans have incredibly low interest rates and longer repayment terms than most other business loans. To me, and a lot of my clients, it's worth the paperwork... all of which you're learning here anyway.)

Now, there is an upside to all of this.

The good thing about a business loan is that it doesn't get reported to your personal credit report, nor does it affect your personal credit score. This means you could conceivably get a business loan, and if need be, a personal loan or additional business/personal credit later on.

Personal credit cards vs. Business credit cards

I always recommend that Funding Preppers be open to utilizing both business and personal credit cards.

Business cards are great because they tend to offer higher limits than personal cards. Why? Because banks understand that running a business requires more capital. And if you've had a business for 2+ years, even better. Banks know that you're more established and are likely bringing in enough revenue to support higher limits.

Business credit cards also tend to be easier to get than business loans, even if you have a brand-new business.

And lastly, some business cards don't appear on your personal credit. This means you'll have some wiggle room to hold balances for a period of time without it affecting your personal credit profile.

However, just because a business card doesn't report to your personal credit doesn't mean that the damage you do goes unnoticed. Some business cards report to your business credit reports or the SBFE. I'll cover this in depth a little later.

But let's not totally rule out personal cards in a business scenario.

Personal credit cards are great because you likely already have some. And if you already have personal credit cards, you could possibly get a boost by asking for a credit limit increase. (As long as it's a soft inquiry!) This gives you some extra money to work with, just for asking.

If you're just starting a business, personal credit cards may be easier to get than business credit. There are even a few credit cards that will tell you the amount of money you've been approved for before you accept the hard inquiry on your credit. (I call these banks *Revealers* in LocateYourLender.com.)

And in case you're wondering about mixing and mingling personal funds with your business, there's a way to do it so that you don't run into any problems with the IRS. I'll talk about that in Part 5.

Think like a lender when structuring your business

It doesn't matter if you're in the planning phase or generating brisk sales, there are certain key elements that every business needs to have in place before they're truly ready to apply for funding.

This is important, even for those of you who have been in business for a while. A business that comes to the funding table with longevity is great. But that longevity only works in your favor if your business is structured properly. Otherwise, those months or years mean nothing. Structure reduces risk.

You'll need to have all these pieces in place before you apply for business funding. It's not optional. These are must-haves. In a lender's mind, this is what separates the toddlers from the teens.

1) **Be a U.S. based business.** You can't get funding if your company is set-up outside of the United States. You can have foreign branches, but you must be formally organized in the States. And that brings me to #2...

2) **Use a commercial address as your business address on all legal documents.** This means, no using your home address as your business address. No P.O. Boxes or UPS store mailboxes either.

   You'll either need a full-time office or storefront, an address at a co-working space or virtual office space like Opus VO. (I specifically mention Opus VO because they'll report your payments to your business credit reports. I'll talk about them later in the *Think Like a Lender When Building Business Credit Scores* section.)

   If you opt for the co-working or virtual office space, make sure you're getting two key services -- an address where you can receive mail, and a phone number with a live receptionist during business hours, as well as voicemail after hours. The receptionist will be able to patch calls through to any number that you designate, and it will give your business a more professional appearance.

   However, I would say that it's better to have dedicated office space, rather than virtual, if you rely on local clientele visiting your place of business. This is especially true when you want to attract clients through the Google 3 Pack, which are the local business listings seen on the first page of Google search results.

Google can be very stringent about who gets airtime in the Google 3 Pack. They've been known to eliminate businesses that don't have dedicated office or retail space.

For all of these reasons, if you're already using your home address for the business, change it. Period. As you continue creating a business structure that's conducive for high-limit funding, you'll see that a business address is a necessity in many different places.

Just know that it's going to take roughly three months to change everything from a home address to a new business address. You'll be switching all the paper trails associated with your company including, registrations at the Secretary of State, the IRS, your bank, as well as address changes that need to take place on your business credit report.

3) **Have a legal structure for your business.** It doesn't matter if it's an LLC, C-Corp or an S-Corp, as long as it's one of these.

This means, if you're currently a sole proprietor, you'll need to register with your Secretary of State as a single-member LLC, S-Corp or C-Corp. And if you have a partnership, I'd suggest a Member Managed LLC, S-Corp or C-Corp, depending on your current revenue.

Each legal structure has its own pros and cons, which is beyond the scope of this book. But a good ole Google search, or a chat with your accountant can help you decide what's best for you... especially from a tax benefit standpoint.

And FYI, it's not that you can't get any funding with a sole proprietorship or a partnership. The problem is that you're limited to only a select few options on the business side.

Furthermore, the crazier the economy gets, with talks of recessions or bubbles bursting; the more lenders prefer to deal with legally structured businesses.

4) **Be registered with the Secretary of State for at least 30 days.** When lenders say that you must have been in business for a specific amount of time, your business's registration date on the Secretary of State website is how they'll gauge that timeframe.

When you start applying for business loans, lines of credit and even net 30 vendor tradelines, the length of time you've been in business will really come into play.

5) **Get an EIN.** An Employee Identification Number (EIN), otherwise known as a Federal Tax Identification Number, can be easily obtained through the IRS website. The IRS uses EIN's to identify businesses for tax purposes. If you plan on hiring employees, operate as a corporation, or meet one of several other requirements, you'll need an EIN.

Once your legal business structure is established, an EIN can be used to open a business bank account, business credit cards, and loans.

6) **Setup a professional website, email address and social media accounts.** If you're going to apply for a business loan, this is a must. Remember the whole risk conversation we've been having this entire time?

This is one of those times when lenders look at much more than just your credit profile. If you're asking for a loan that's greater than six-figures, then you better believe you're going to be scrutinized.

Lenders will look at where your office or storefront is located on Google Maps. They will check out your website. They'll see what's happening on your social media accounts. If you're using a Gmail address, it should be directly tied to your company's domain. So, no to (*JanesCookies6358@gmail.com*), and yes to (*Jane@JanesCookies.com*).

7) **Get your business listed in local online directories.** This step is necessary for two reasons.

   Having your business in online directories shows lenders that you're established and actively vetting for business. It's an easy way to show that you're not a risk. Secondly, if you're trying to get your business listed in the Google 3-Pack, you must have citations -- which are basically listings in business directories.

   There are easily 200+ business directories that you can submit your info to. This is why it's so vital that you have a commercial address already established. You obviously don't want your home address floating around hundreds of online directories.

   Furthermore, your business name, address and phone number must be the same in every business directory. This is known as NAP (Name, Address, Phone Number), in the online marketing space. If you're using 123 Maple Street, then don't switch and put 123 Maple St. And you don't want to start with 123 Maple Street, and then midway switch to 45 South Main Street. Constant consistency is key.

   Even better, hire someone to do the directory submissions on your behalf. I've listed a few trusted vendors at (FundingPreppers.com/BookLinks).

8) **Request business reviews.** If you already have an established business, you're probably already receiving reviews from customers. And that's fabulous because lenders love to see reviews. The more, the better. The newer, even better

   Not only that, Google's 3-Pack gives preference to businesses that are popular. Reviews are a clear-cut way to boost popularity. I won't go into detail on how to do reputation management. But you should have a plan on getting reviews from customers.

The high-level view of how lenders judge your businesses fundability

There are seven primary questions every lender will ask when you apply for funding in your company name.

These may not be the only questions they ask, but they're usually baked in to the first line of assessment. Even when you apply for a business credit card, these questions form the criteria for acceptance.

- ⊙ **What business are you in?** Your industry matters. Not every lender will lend to every industry. Some industries are considered high risk, and you'll need to look for personal credit or personal loans, rather than business loans. I'll cover this in a bit.

- ⊙ **How long have you been in business?** Businesses go through growth cycles. Your place within the growth cycle often determines how stable (or risky) your business is. The length of time you've been in business may also determine whether you're eligible for specific forms of funding.

- ⊙ **How much monthly revenue is your business bringing in?** Lenders need to see that you're earning enough revenue to cover repayment of the loan. Additionally, they're assessing where your funds are originating from. For instance, if more than 30% of your business income is derived from a single client, that's a red flag for a lender... particularly SBA lenders. After all, what happens if that client leaves you?

- ⊙ **How much funding do you need, and what do you need it for?** Companies in your industry have a standard for how much money they request and why they're requesting it. Your requests should mirror that. It doesn't matter how beautiful and insightful your business plan is... it's still going to look really odd if you're asking for $600,000 to open a little cactus kiosk at the mall. But if you say you need $15,000 to stock up on cactus planters for the holiday season, that's a reasonable request based on what lenders know about the retail holiday season.

⊙ **What does your business credit look like?** There are four business credit scores that lenders may review. I'll talk about them a little later in this chapter.

⊙ **What does your personal credit look like?** Whether you're applying for a business loan or credit card, nearly every lender is going to look at your personal credit, specifically because you're a small business owner.

⊙ **What is your DTI ratio?** Whenever you apply for unsecured funding (a loan or credit that doesn't require collateral) lenders want to see your debt-to-income ratio. I spoke about calculating your personal DTI ratio in the previous chapter. But I'll also give you the logistics of figuring out your businesses DTI in Part 3.

Think like a lender when looking at how risky your industry is

No matter what industry you're in, you're a risk to a lender.

However, there are certain types of businesses that tend to stick out as being *above average* in the risk category. And even in the *above average* category, there are still some businesses that are so risky, neither conventional nor alternative lenders will touch them.

I imagine that most business owners know when they're in a high-risk sector because it'll be difficult for you to get a basic merchant credit card processing account. If PayPal and Stripe won't deal with your type of business, there's a good chance other lenders will be just as apprehensive. That's an 'in-the-trenches' way of knowing that you're *above average* risk.

There are six general standards that point to a high-risk business. If you're in one of these categories, believe me when I say that it's going to be a lot more difficult (if not impossible) to get business funding.

In this case, you have two options. Accept the fact that you'll only be using personal credit or personal loans. Or book a consultation with me at FundingPreppers.com. I work with a lot of different lenders, so I'm always keeping an eye out for lenders that deal with non-traditional and high-risk borrowers.

And if you're thinking about starting a new business, consider these options as the water you don't want to swim in.

1. **Businesses that have strict licensing and compliance laws are typically high risk.**

    Adult-themed businesses, drugs/pharmaceuticals/tobacco, alcohol, weapons and firearms, and gambling businesses must all follow strict laws. These groups are automatically high risk, even if you're following the letter of the law.

    For example, a cannabis-related business has rigorous state and federal laws that it must follow. Not surprisingly, it's hard for cannabis businesses to get funding (but not impossible).

2. **Money related businesses are high risk and typically DO NOT receive any type of funding.** Rare coin dealers fall under this category... accounting firms, insurance companies, finance companies, leasing companies, currency exchangers, and loan brokers do not receive funding.

3. **Businesses that historically generate a large number of chargebacks or provide dubious products/services are considered high risk.** Lenders refer to MLM/network marketing businesses, ponzi schemes, and get rich quick products as high risk. Sorry to those of you who are in the

network marketing business, but yeah, it is an industry that the FTC keeps a close eye on. That means, no business loans.

Under that *'dubious'* definition, let's say for example, you sell knock-off luxury goods -- like fake Gucci purses. You're not going to get funding. If it's an attempt to deceive the buyer, it's dubious and not fundable.

4. **Businesses that have a lot of competitors, like nail salons, restaurants and even retail stores are high risk.** In this case, however, it's not impossible for Main Street businesses to get funding. And by Main Street, I mean local brick-and-mortar businesses.

   I've directed many Main Street clients to micro and community-based lenders. Just keep your expectations reasonable. You're not going to get a $100,000 loan from a community-based lender to open a nail salon.

5. **Seasonal businesses and those with inconsistent cash flow are also in the high-risk category.** A lawn care business within a geographic area that has long, snowy winters can be seen as high risk because they're only in business for part of the year.

   As far as inconsistent cash flow, restaurants and even trucking and transportation businesses fall into this category. You can still get money if you're in an industry known for inconsistent cash flow, it just may not be a traditional term business loan.

6. **Businesses that offer products/services that will be used in the distant future.** This would include any type of membership services greater than 12 months in the future like travel services, fitness clubs/gyms, and membership-type services or groups.

If your business belongs to any of the categories listed below, securing a business loan or credit card is generally NOT possible.

⊙ Adult entertainment

⊙ Alcohol

⊙ Pharmaceuticals/tobacco

⊙ Gambling

⊙ Firearms/weapons

⊙ MLM

⊙ Get rich quick

⊙ Dubious products (i.e., knock-off purses)

⊙ Any money related service (including cryptocurrency)

However, if your business is a:

⊙ Membership-based product or service (like a fitness center)

⊙ Cannabis/CBD business

⊙ Competition intense business (i.e., retail store or restaurant)

… you may have trouble getting funding through traditional brand-name banks, like Bank of America or Wells Fargo. But rest assured there are smaller, independent lenders that are willing to work with those in riskier industries.

Just keep in mind, these loans may come with higher interest rates, an origination fee, or terms that require weekly/bi-weekly payments. In other words, funding for risky industries typically have extra fees automatically included.

> *Reader Question… "If I'm in a risky industry, and I change my business name to something more generic sounding, would that be a good way to avoid being flagged as a risky business?"*

This is a gray area. In some very limited situations, you can do this.

But I'm just going to say early on that ultimately, I don't think it's worth it.

Yes, your business name can showcase the type of business you're running. For example, we don't have to think too hard to know that Bill's Barbershop is a place where people go to get a haircut. The name just says it all.

But even if it didn't... even if Bill's Barbershop was named Bill's Spot, which doesn't directly show that it's a barbershop... your business name is just one thing that a lender looks at when determining what type of business, you're in.

It's not just about the name of the business.

A lender can determine what type of business you're in by looking at a few things:

1. **Your NAICS code** - NAICS stands for North American Industry Classification Code. The main purpose of this classification system is so that banks, the IRS, vendors and lenders can easily identify the type of business you're running.

   Now here comes the important part. And I'm getting this directly from the NAICS website: *"The system was developed for statistical analysis, however, various government agencies, trade associations, and regulatory boards have adapted the NAICS classification system for their internal needs."*

   This means, if you run a trucking business (which you already know is considered high risk) you should be using the appropriate NAICS code for insurance purposes.

   Outside of a trucking business, if you need certain licenses to start or run the business, you may not want to BS with your NAICS code. You just never know how it could potentially affect your business in the future.

But it doesn't end there.

When you sign up for a business bank account, the bank is going to ask for your NAICS code. Same when you get your EIN number from the IRS.

This means if you've already established your business in the eyes of the IRS and a bank, changing the name of your business won't make a difference. Your NAICS code is already a dead giveaway.

However, if you haven't started your business yet, and it's fluid enough to be classified under more than one NAICS code, you *may* be able to choose your code in an area that's off the risky radar.

For example, if you do credit repair IN ADDITION TO business consulting, then you could honestly choose the NAICS code for Management, Scientific, and Technical Consulting Services.

2. **A lender can also look at your IRS records to determine what kind of business you're in.**

How?

Well, there are specific deductions that are common and expected for certain types of businesses.

For instance, if you run a trucking business, your taxes may show deductions for things like commercial liability insurance, dispatch fees, load expenses, driver meals, and so on.

Therefore, if your business name is something generic like Thomas Enterprises... and your NAICS code is 484121 (which is the general freight trucking code) AND your taxes are showing trucking-business expenses, the lender is going to know that you run a trucking business, even if you say it's a consulting business.

3. **A lender can look at your bank statements.** Going back to the Thomas Enterprises trucking business, your bank statements show things like: payments to gas credit cards, commercial insurance debits, payments to industry associations, and maybe payments to truck rental companies.

If you're selling women's jewelry, your bank statements might show consistent purchases from wholesale jewelry websites. In that case, even if your business is named Valerie Enterprises, it's going to be apparent that you're most likely selling jewelry.

And it works the same way if you run a service business. Your bank account can reveal certain details about insurance and licensing costs, trade organizations you're a member of and events you attend. Trucking insurance costs are going to look very different from liability insurance for a business consulting firm.

As you can see, even though there are small ways to kinda 'not' showcase your business as being risky, it may be virtually impossible if your business is already established.

While changing your business name sounds enticing and is do-able, it may not totally mask who you are and what you sell. My suggestion -- and I said this before -- is that you always keep it honest. Recognize your limitations and work within those parameters.

Every entrepreneur is a serial entrepreneur. If you can't use all of this advice for an existing business, I'm sure it'll be usable for a future idea.

Think like a lender when looking at your existing business revenue

When it comes to business funding, your revenue can open a lot of doors.

You're going to have the best possible offers if your revenue is over $10,000 a month. However, your business could be bringing in as little as $3,000 a month, and you could still get funded.

Low revenue does not exclude you from the funding table. But if you do have low revenue – (and by 'low' I mean under $10,000 a month) – then understand that lending decisions will be made on your entire financial profile, not just your revenue.

Lower revenue means lenders will look more intensely...

- ⊙ At your personal credit profile,
- ⊙ At your business credit profile,
- ⊙ At how much money you need.

Let's say your business is bringing in $3,000 a month. If your credit scores are in the 750-ish range, your utilization is below 4%, and you have seven solid accounts on your business credit reports, you could qualify for a business credit card with a $5,000-$10,000 limit, or a merchant cash advance (which is like a loan) for around $1,000.

Even if you throw in $8,700 a month from your day job as part of your income, you still wouldn't get more money. (Personal income from your job isn't counted towards business revenue.) But you may be able to get a $20,000 personal loan, or even a credit card for that amount, if you used your job income and your business revenue on a personal funding application.

But if you were to come to the table with that same $3,000 a month, 605-ish FICO 8 scores and no business credit, expecting a $10,000 business loan or even that much in business credit cards, you'd be

71

denied and disappointed. Those low credit scores mean you'd need to temper your expectations about the amount of money you'd get.

Case in point, a few years ago, I worked with Kathy, a Shopify store owner who had been in business for 11 months. She was bringing in roughly $3,000-$4,000 a month. Her personal FICO 8 credit scores were 618, 627, and 620.

I recommended that Kathy get funding in her business's name because her personal credit was still shaky. My goal was to start her business funding journey with a lender that she could grow with as her credit improved.

At that time, I was able to get her a $1,500 merchant cash advance.

And in case you're unfamiliar, a merchant cash advance isn't a loan. It's an advance against your future revenue. You make payments toward the advance either daily or weekly.

Now here's the truth... merchant cash advances don't provide the best funding terms and the APR can be hella ugly when compared to a traditional term loan. (There's no sugarcoating that part!) But if your revenue is low and your personal credit is holding on by a thread, a merchant cash advance may be your best source of business funding.

And that's okay! Do not let the "bad credit option" deter you.

I always tell my credit-troubled clients to think long term. And thinking long term means you'll sometimes have to take a crappy loan from a good lender on the front end to prove that you're not a risk. Once you've gotten over that hurdle, it's easier to ask for more money and better terms – even if your personal credit is still in the recovery phase.

Kathy's profile presented enough risk that I knew she wouldn't get a traditional loan.

⊙ She had 2 late payments on her personal credit, that were both under 24 months old. These are still considered relatively new. In fact, any derogatory marks that are under 2 years old have the most point draining power on your credit scores.

  If these late payments were 5-6 years old, and she had no other problems, then maybe she'd have a chance elsewhere. But when they're 2 years or under, you've got to have significant revenue to offset those derogatory marks.

⊙ She had high utilization on her credit cards... 69% to be exact. If she had $100,000 in available credit, 69% utilization would mean she had $69,000 in balances.

  In Part 1, I mentioned that FICO recommends a utilization of under 30%. I tell Funding Preppers that under 6% is typically that sweet spot where you'll see the highest limits.

  These two factors contributed to her 'slightly less than okay' FICO scores.

⊙ She didn't have any business credit at that time. And now with those late payments, it would be harder for her to get high-limit business cards if the banks were to check her personal credit. (Which they almost always do, nowadays.)

⊙ And finally, her business was bringing in less than $10,000 a month. She has never even hit that threshold. While her business revenue or lack of business credit isn't affecting her credit scores, the combination of all these factors did affect her chances of getting a sizable loan amount.

With the overall view of Kathy's financial profile, I suggested the merchant cash advance. She took it. She paid it off. She got a second merchant cash advance and paid that one off as well. Over the years she has been rebuilding her personal credit and building her business credit using the Pinnacle Score Pathway, which you'll learn about later in this chapter.

And now, more than three years later, her business is bringing in $26,000-$35,000 a month. Kathy was able to get a $40,000 loan from the same lender who started her off with those merchant cash advances.

I frequently hear business owners say that you should have a relationship with a bank before you ask for funding. The thing is, this is even more true if you're working on rebuilding your credit. Having a relationship with a lender that caters to business owners with good and bad credit can be a serious asset.

Now let's look at it from a different angle.

Alex came to me looking for a $10,000 loan to purchase inventory for the upcoming holiday season.

He had been in business for 14 months... monthly revenue was around $17,000... FICO 8's ranged from 711-724. He had no derogatory accounts, no late payments, and his utilization was at 22%. He was right in the middle of building his business credit profile using the Pinnacle Score Pathway, so he only had 1 financial tradeline and 2 vendor tradelines showing. No major business credit cards.

Since Alex was looking to purchase inventory, I suggested that he ditch the loan request and consider an income-based credit card or a line of credit.

A loan would only be good for this one season, whereas a credit card or a line of credit could be used again and again during subsequent holidays when he needed to increase his inventory spend.

He agreed and decided to take a chance with an income-based credit card. The result was a $22,000 starting limit.

Since it was a personal credit card and he was using it to buy inventory, I suggested that he only use it for business purposes. This way, when tax season rolled around, there was no co-mingling of business and personal funds. (Sometimes you gotta think like a lender, and sometimes you gotta think like an accountant.)

How you receive your revenue is just as important as how much that revenue is

The #1 reason why Alex was able to receive that $22,000 credit card is because of how he banked his income from the business.

He used Stripe and PayPal to receive credit card payments from customers. Those payments went directly into his business bank account.

From that business revenue, he used ADP to pay himself a salary. (ADP is a payroll processing service that takes a pre-determined portion of your revenue and pays you a salary.)

That money, which is his personal salary for running the company, was then direct deposited into his personal bank account.

So now he has income being deposited into both his business and personal checking accounts.

If Alex wants business funding, he's got a business income paper trail. And if he wants to buy a house, or a car, or get a student loan for his son, he's got a personal income paper trail as well.

This exact type of cashflow configuration will be a huge blessing when you're trying to get funding.

Speaking of a paper trail, lenders are starting to slowly veer away from requesting paper paystubs for income verification. Instead, they're connecting directly to your bank account with services like Plaid, to verify your income.

What is "Plaid," you ask?

Plaid is a widely used fintech (financial technology) service that allows lenders to see your bank account activity including incoming revenue, deposits, debits, withdrawals and overdrafts. It basically eliminates lenders having to ask for bank statements or paystubs to confirm your cashflow.

Plaid can be used on both business and personal checking accounts, and lenders will present the option during the application process – or not. Just depends on the lender and the product you're applying for.

When you're applying for business funding, you'll use a special link to connect Plaid to your business bank account. And if you're like Alex who was applying for a personal credit card, you'll connect Plaid to your personal checking account.

Now let's say you go to Bank A, only Bank A will be able to see your bank account data at that time. If you apply to Bank B, and Bank B also requests access through Plaid, then Bank B will be able to see your account as well. But if you have accounts at Banks C and D, they will not have Plaid access. You must give each lender individual permission to access your account, and Plaid only shows your account activity to lenders as they request it.

Either way, I know this process may seem invasive. However, you never have to agree to a Plaid connection. You can always say "no."

But that doesn't mean a lender will give you other verification options. Sometimes they will, and sometimes they won't. As times are changing, again, it just depends on the lender.

I recently applied for a line of credit and declined the Plaid connection. The lender did give me the option to submit paystubs, and I did that instead. Long story short, the lender claimed they couldn't verify the validity of the paystubs and they still wanted Plaid access.

At that point, I let them in. Within 30 seconds, they verified my info, and I was immediately approved for $41,000.

This is also how Alex was able to quickly get approved for that $22,000 credit card. The lender used Plaid to access his personal checking account, where he had been receiving consistent paychecks from his company. His personal credit profile was important, but it was his income that jump started the credit limit.

So, take it for what it is. Like it, love it, or hate it... Plaid isn't going anywhere. It's one of those 'assimilate-now-or-assimilate-later' situations.

Plus, as someone who works with a lot of lenders, I appreciate the fact that Plaid prevents applicants from being able to play Doctor Photoshop on their bank statements. In that regard, it ends up being much faster and easier to approve someone when Plaid provides account confirmation.

Think like a lender when paying yourself

In this section, I'd like to take revenue in a new direction -- namely in the form of an owner's salary.

Once your business is generating $5,000-$10,000 a month, you should pay yourself on a consistent and regular basis. And you'll do it the way your accountant will love you, with payroll taxes taken out, direct deposits, and a W-2 issued for the year.

From a funding standpoint, an owner's salary shows business lenders that your company is financially stable. Remember, our goal is to always reduce risk. And issuing yourself a salary is a great way to do that.

But more than that, as you've seen from Alex's story, giving yourself a salary also opens more *personal* funding opportunities.

And it all starts with how you list your employment status on your funding applications.

If you're receiving a regular paycheck from your business, I suggest you list yourself as 'Employed' instead of 'Self-Employed,' on your personal credit card and personal loan applications.

Listing yourself as 'Self-Employed' on a personal credit card, personal loan, or even a mortgage application, sometimes causes your application to be flagged. If an application isn't flagged, it often gets automatically approved.

But when it's flagged, you could be forced to submit additional documentation. Your application is often scrutinized more under the Self-Employed status. I don't know if the additional scrutiny affects your limits one way or the other. But I do know that it's better to produce as few red flags as possible. We're always trying to avoid being seen as a risk.

Listing yourself as 'Employed,' is perfectly legal because if the business is paying you a regular salary, then you ARE an employee.

Your business' legal structure dictates how you should pay yourself

An LLC, S-Corp or C-Corp is its own entity. The company is like your child. You may have started it, but once you give it life with a legal structure, the company is totally separate from you.

This means the business bank account shouldn't be treated like it's your personal bank account, because technically it's not. Taking a salary from the company is an important distinction.

Even if it's a one-person company, you should be receiving a *reasonable* salary. And by *reasonable*, I mean your salary should be in line with what others in your field receive, otherwise you'll get into trouble with the IRS over payroll taxes.

In fact, if your business is structured as an S-Corp or a C-Corp, you're supposed to receive a salary. That's because when S-Corp or C-Corp shareholders (owners) perform regular work for the business, they are considered employees.

Owner's draw vs Salary

If your business is structured as an LLC, you can either opt for an owner's draw (which is applicable in most states), or you can take a reasonable salary.

When you take an owner's draw, you're basically giving yourself profits from the LLC.

In the case of a single-member LLC, you can take as much as you want as an owner's draw, provided you leave enough in the business bank account for operating expenses. In other words, you cannot drain your business bank account dry.

If it's a multi-member LLC, you must have the conditions for an owner's draw outlined in the Operating Agreement. At that point, you and your business partners can do an owner's draw.

When you're trying to decide whether you should do an owner's draw or a salary, there are a couple things to consider.

An owner's draw makes sense when your LLC is new or if the business's income isn't consistent. For example, if the business brought in $2,000 in May, $400 in June, and $1,300 in July, a salary wouldn't make sense.

However, the problem with an owner's draw is that it doesn't show lenders consistent income like a salary would. If you were applying for a personal credit card, and a lender checked your income using Plaid, they'd see that it's sporadic when you're just doing owner's drawers. Sporadic income makes you look riskier than someone who has a consistent paycheck.

On the other hand, if you have several $10,000+ months, and cash flow is steadily on the incline, a salary would be appropriate and recommended. Salaries decrease risk.

And if you want to make your financial life a lot easier, use a payroll service to issue your salary. Yup, even if you're just a one-person operation.

A payroll company does all the heavy lifting.

- ⊙ They take care of all the payroll taxes,
- ⊙ They do all the W-2 form filing and distribution,
- ⊙ And they'll direct deposit your money into your bank account (just like a regular job).

I promise you, knowing that your payroll is done right will easily stave off 15 headaches and 297 cuss words every month. The benefits are totally worth the small cost.

And just in case you're curious about the cost, at the time that I'm writing this book, Roll (by ADP) charges $29 a month, plus $4 per employee.

You can't beat it y'all. Salary up!

Think like a lender when explaining your funding needs

If you run a retail shop on Main Street, lenders know what you may need funding for. Same, if you run a law firm, manufacture air fresheners, or run a 100-acre pecan farm.

Each business is part of a specific industry. And each industry has its own funding needs that are unique to businesses within that industry.

If you're getting a business loan, and the lender asks, "*What are you going to use this money for?*" you need to provide an answer that makes sense for businesses in your industry. You also need to map out the potential risks involved, and how you aim to avoid those risks.

This is important! Sometimes when business owners come to me to help them find a lender, they don't have a concrete response to this question.

Often, they'll say something like, *"Well, I need the money to grow my business."*

To which I'll respond, *"Great! What are you doing to grow your business? What would the money go towards?"*

Applicants who reply with specific details get funded a lot quicker than those who haven't sufficiently mapped out a plan. A plan removes some of the risk. It shows that you've considered how you'll grow the business. You're actively watching the meter.

The right way to explain your funding needs

Bill recently came to me because he needed a loan for a big piece of construction equipment.

There were 8 sizable construction jobs in his area coming up. All of those jobs required the piece of equipment that Bill wanted. He also knew that only 2 of the local contracting companies had this particular piece of equipment. He knew (because he'd lost previous bids) that it would be easier for him to get these jobs if he had this machine.

The whole story made sense to me. He had a reason why he needed the funds. His company had experience in the field. He had proof regarding the upcoming jobs.

And when I asked him what would happen if he bid on those 8 jobs and didn't get any, he explained that he could rent out the piece of equipment to companies that got the job. Basically, Bill was showing me that he had at least one way to mitigate the risk.

Not only that... it takes us back to the 5 C's of credit.

When a lender asks, *"What do you need the money for?"*, one of the things they're looking at is the *Conditions* surrounding your industry.

In Bill's case, there were several construction jobs coming up that his company was qualified to handle. He was already working two other jobs in the area. A lender would see that Bill was active in that arena.

Now let's say you're asking for a loan for your costume jewelry store on Amazon.

A lender would know that you need inventory. They'll know that you'll need to really stock up before key holidays like Christmas, Valentine's Day and Mother's Day. They'll also know that if you don't sell that inventory because it's outdated or ugly, it could be harder for you to pay that loan back.

They know the conditions for needing the loan, and they also know the risks involved. How can you show them that you're not going to pose a risk?

You would be wise to come with sales records from your Amazon portal. You should have a direct link to your Amazon store so they can see your customer reviews. You must also be prepared to explain what you're going to do with that inventory if it doesn't sell.

Are you going to slash prices and have a big sale on your website? Will you sell it to a liquidation house? Do you have an email list of avid costume jewelry buyers?

Keep in mind, not all lenders will ask these questions. I tend to lean on the side of over-planning. But the benefit of thinking in depth like this is that if something should actually go wrong, you already have a plan to keep your head above water.

We know that 50% of businesses fail within the first 5 years. However, I'm willing to bet that if more business owners thought about and planned for downfalls, that there would be far fewer failures.

Identifying your business's industry

Every business fits into one of these 6 industries.

1. Retailing

2. Wholesaling

3. Manufacturing

4. Construction

5. Services

6. Agricultural

If you're selling non-prescription eyewear on an ecommerce website, your business falls under the *retailing* industry.

If you're purchasing pallets of non-prescription eyewear from a manufacturer and selling it to retailers, then you're in the *wholesale* industry.

If you own a factory that makes eyeglass frames from raw materials, your business is in the *manufacturing* industry.

If your company physically builds factories from the ground up, you're in the *construction* industry.

If you have a staffing company that provides construction workers to building projects, you're in the *services* industry.

And if you grow apples that get sold at construction sites, your business is in the *agricultural* industry.

Businesses in a specific industry have similar funding needs

As I mentioned before, when you go to a business lender, they expect to see certain things about your business based on the industry you're in.

This section will help you understand what lenders already know, so that you can formulate a plan to show that you're aware of the risks and ready to handle them.

RETAILING INDUSTRY

A lender who deals with retailers is going to know that:

⊙ Your biggest asset is your inventory, and if you run a brick-and-mortar business, your fixtures. If you have a brick-and-mortar storefront, real estate you own is seen as an asset and possibly collateral.

⊙ Lenders know that you'll need extra inventory during holidays or seasonal events.

⊙ They know that if you buy excess inventory, it may go obsolete or off-trend before you have a chance to sell it -- that's a risk.

⊙ They know that if there are a small number of wholesalers in your niche, the lack of wholesaler diversity could eventually impact your retail sales.

⊙ They know if you don't ship your orders in a timely fashion, you'll get bad reviews, which could lead to reduced sales. In fact, retail and ecommerce lenders look for your store reviews as part of their background check.

⊙ They know that depending on the size or location of your business, you may encounter a certain amount of employee or customer theft.

Be prepared to answer the following questions:

- ⊙ How strong is the demand for your products? What's the average order amount? Has that increased or decreased over time?

- ⊙ What have previous holiday sales numbers looked like? Are you selling out of product, or do you have to liquidate after the holiday?

- ⊙ How quickly do you turnover your inventory? A high turnover indicates strong sales. This is a vital metric for inventory loans, in particular.

- ⊙ What kind of reviews do you have? What do customers say about your products? Do you have a Net Promote score? This isn't the most important factor, but it does contribute to the Character portion of the 5 C's of credit.

WHOLESALING INDUSTRY

Lenders that deal with wholesalers will already know that:

- ⊙ Your strongest assets are inventory and accounts receivables. A secondary asset would be owned real estate, like warehouse space.

- ⊙ They know that your liabilities may include: the quality of the goods purchased, your credit policy, and your ability to find and sell to retailers.

- ⊙ Purchasing too much of a product and not being able to sell it to retailers can be detrimental to small wholesalers. This is clearly a risk.

- ⊙ You likely need funding to purchase inventory, equipment, fixtures, and for real estate acquisition.

Be prepared to answer the following questions:

- ⊙ How much of your accounts receivable is outstanding? A lender that sees too many 60–90 day invoices will know that you have a collection problem. You need to work on that part before you get funding. Pouring money into the business isn't going to fix that underlying issue.

- ⊙ How quickly is your inventory being turned over? To figure this out, you'll need to calculate the inventory turnover ratio, which tells lenders the length of time it takes to sell your inventory within a specific period.

MANUFACTURING INDUSTRY

A manufacturing business could be as small as a one-person operation making stick-on decals from their garage... to a warehouse operation stitching pricey underwear... up to a multi-building complex bottling organic juices. Regardless of where you are on that scale, a lender who works with manufacturing businesses knows:

- ⊙ Your most valuable assets are inventory, accounts receivables, equipment and machinery, or the plant where products are made.

- ⊙ Your business will always need raw or partially built materials.

- ⊙ Your financial success is directly tied to how efficient your manufacturing process is. If your manufacturing process is slow, this is going to impact sales.

- ⊙ They know that two of your biggest risks are: purchasing raw materials of poor quality and not being able to sell inventory in a timely fashion. Manufactured products that sit too long can expire or become outdated.

- ⊙ They know that unpaid account receivables may point to an overly lenient credit extension policy. In other words, you're not collecting money from wholesalers or retailers quick enough.

- And they know that your funding needs will often entail raw material purchases, plant, property and equipment purchases, as well as carrying account receivables.

Be prepared for lenders to ask the following questions:

- How quickly do you collect on account receivables? Do you provide credit terms of net 15, net 30 or greater? If your account receivables are too late, the lender will suggest that you improve your collection process.

- How are you handling the accounts payables. Are you buying on credit? Are you making and selling the product, then paying for raw materials? Or is your money tied up in inventory that hasn't sold yet?

- How quickly are you able to turnover inventory? Do you have a wait list of customers? Do you need more warehouse space because your existing inventory isn't moving quickly?

CONSTRUCTION INDUSTRY

If you're in a construction-related business, like contracting, a lender is going to know that:

- Your accounts receivables are likely your company's biggest assets - but they can also be heavy liabilities, if your clients don't pay on time.

- Depending on the type of company you run, your machinery and heavy equipment may be a sizable asset - (and this is important because equipment can sometimes be used as collateral).

- Your business hinges on the cost and quality of your labor force and materials. Crappy workers + crappy materials = crappy work + big liabilities.

- If you're underbidding on jobs, this could leave your profit margins razor thin.

- Adverse weather conditions can slow business down dramatically if much of your work is done outside.

- If you're asking for a loan, you likely need the funding to pay workers, to purchase materials, to purchase big equipment, or even for a standby letter of credit.

Be prepared to answer the following questions:

- How much of your account receivables are outstanding? Lenders want to see how quickly you're paid, and how much you're owed. When you have too many late invoices, lenders will usually advise you to fix your collection problems first.

- What kind of heavy machinery/equipment do you have? How old is it? What kind of condition is it in? Are you still financing it? Depending on your situation, heavy machinery could be used as collateral.

SERVICE INDUSTRY

Since service businesses don't provide an actual product, your funding needs are going to be different than those of product-based businesses. You may need to seek lenders that specialize in your particular type of business. For example, there are lenders for medical practices, lenders for law firms, and so on.

Either way, there are some general things service-based lenders will know:

- That your biggest assets are accounts receivables -- (money owed to you), any owned business real estate, intellectual property, patents/copyrights, or even your equipment. For example, a medical practice may provide patient care -- which is a service. But they may need specialty equipment to provide the service.

⊙ Employees can make or break your business. This is especially true if the service you provide requires specialist knowledge or licensing.

⊙ New government and compliance regulations can put financial pressure on your business.

⊙ Business reviews, be they good or bad, can affect your bottom line. So, if you have a ton of bad reviews, this will affect your ability to secure funding.

⊙ When you ask for funding, it may be needed for office space, advertising/marketing costs, hiring new staff, or compliance upgrades.

Be prepared to answer the following questions:

⊙ What is your accounts receivable cycle? Net 15... net 30... or greater?

⊙ Do you have a business plan that shows the demand for your type of service? This is especially true if your business is geographically locked.

⊙ Do you have patents or trademarks? In this case, they want to see things that make you legally solid within your industry.

AGRICULTURAL INDUSTRY

If you're on the farming side of the agricultural industry, you're likely going to work with ag focused lenders, which is short for agricultural lenders.

That's because farmers have unique needs as compared to other types of industries. For example, an agricultural loan may not require monthly payments. Loans may be paid once crops or livestock are sold off.

If your business is in the agricultural industry, but it's not necessarily counted as a farm, your funding options may be more open. Either way, the lender will know that:

- ⊙ Your biggest assets are equipment, real estate/land, and even livestock.

- ⊙ Weather conditions can greatly affect agricultural businesses in your geographic area.

- ⊙ One of your biggest expenses is finding and keeping reliable labor. If you have a farming compound, you may need to house laborers on site.

- ⊙ The older your equipment, the higher the maintenance costs may be. Whereas the newer your business, the more likely you'll need to purchase equipment. And if you already have equipment, how viable of an asset is it? Can it be used as collateral?

- ⊙ And finally, they know that your funding needs will center around purchases of seed, feed and livestock, equipment, land/housing, and labor.

Be ready to answer these questions:

- ⊙ What were your crop reports for the previous year, including yield and yield history?

- ⊙ What is your budget and expected cash flow for the upcoming year?

- ⊙ What's your year-end balance sheet showing, as far as: accounts payable/receivables, grain and livestock inventory, as well as a list of long-term assets?

Think like a lender when looking at the length of time you've been in business

Brittany recently called me for a business loan. Pretty early on in our meeting, she emphatically stated that she didn't want any of those 'predatory' business loans.

Of course, I asked, *"What do you mean by predatory business loans?"*

To which she replied, *"Oh, you know... the ones with the high interest rates that you need to pay back weekly. My friend had one and it messed up her credit big time!"*

Rest assured, funding doesn't 'mess up' your credit -- but not paying your debts absolutely will.

And I understand that everybody wants the low-to-no interest funding options, because that's what's heavily advertised by a ton of lenders online.

Realistically though, if you have a young business (under two years old) lenders are going to view it as a risk. And when you add in something like a 610 FICO 8 score, this turns into a situation where your funding options are limited.

On the other hand, if you have a one year old business, but your FICO 8 scores are above 750, and your business revenue is $5,000-$6,000 a month, and you've got three business credit accounts in good standing -- you have a better chance of being approved for more traditional business funding options.

Brittany wasn't in this club!

Her business was six months old with her highest FICO 8 being 607. Business revenue had been holding steady around $4,500 a month for the past three months. She had no business credit.

Guess what she qualified for? A merchant cash advance! She'd only been in business a short period of time, and her low FICO 8s pointed to some unpaid derogatory accounts on her credit report.

I recommended that instead of taking the MCA, she work on building up her business credit and start paying off some of that derogatory debt that was suppressing her credit score. Paying the debt wouldn't remove it. But it would show potential lenders that she was willing to own up to her mistakes.

Anyway, I say all of this to say that the amount of time you've been in business plays a vital role in the funding process, particularly when you're applying for a business loan. To put it bluntly, you can't reasonably expect a term business loan with super sexy terms if you're still in the startup phase.

A startup doesn't have the solid financial history of a company that has been around for several years.

This is why personal credit is such a big deal early on. Having good personal credit won't open all doors -- for instance, you must have been in business for two years to get an SBA 7(a) loan. But it will help you open a lot more doors than if you have fair or bad personal credit.

This is also a huge reason why if you have good credit, I suggest utilizing personal loans and credit during the first two years of growing your business.

And if you're at the helm of a startup business, riding a 600 FICO 8 wave, you may have to take out a crappy business loan now to set the stage for better funding opportunities later. What you do today is going to set the foundation for what you get tomorrow, or next year, or within the next 10 years.

Funding is rarely a one-and-done thing.

Once you realize how massively important it is to be able to hold on to your own money, funding may become an integral part of your business growth.

Look at it as a long-term strategy, with a four-stage life cycle.

Understanding what cycle your business is in will help determine what type of funding you can get.

So, let's talk about those life cycles.

Startup Phase

Your doors are newly opened. The website is up and running. You're trying to figure out everything from marketing and sales to inventory, employee management and all the things in between.

The startup phase is notoriously difficult because there are so many unknown variables at play. Not surprisingly, this is where approximately 50% of all businesses fail.

With those statistics hovering overhead, this is the main reason why business lenders are skittish about lending to businesses at this stage.

Within the first year of launching, your *Capacity* (yup, back to the 5 C's) is limited. This means lenders have little historical information on your business's ability to pay back a loan with your existing business revenue. (Helloooooo personal credit!)

It doesn't mean there's a stop sign when it comes to funding in this phase. It just means your options may not be as plentiful as they would be in the second or third stage of the business life cycle.

Business lenders will usually look at your company as a 'startup' for the first two years you're open. This period begins once your business becomes official through the Secretary of State registration.

Speaking of which, if you are thinking about starting a business or you're still in the early part of the startup phase, this is a great time to either begin pre-planning your funding options for the future, or to start making some course corrections.

This is the time when you want to thoughtfully choose your business bank. Because where you start planting roots now could affect your ability to obtain funding later.

With that said, I don't always recommend bigger, name-brand banks because they're not always the easiest for smaller businesses to get funding from in the future.

Some clients say Bank of America is tight-fisted when it comes to small business loans. I've had clients with well-established businesses, easily run $20,000+ a month through a Bank of America business account, and still get denied a business loan. And then on the flipside, same clients have $20,000-$30,000 credit cards with them. The risk is placed in one financial product, but not another. Go figure!

LocateYourLender.com tells you which banks are ideal for startup businesses that want funding in the future.

Growth Phase

This is where the ball is officially rolling! Your customer base is growing. Profits are no longer a pipe dream, and people are talking about your business (hopefully!) in a positive way.

The SBA places businesses in the Growth stage, starting at the two-year mark. That's when you can apply for an SBA 7(a) loan.

And FYI, this is a completely different, and far more extensive experience than applying for the SBA sponsored PPP and EIDL loans that were available during the height of the COVID pandemic.

Besides the SBA, major financial institutions like Chase and US Bank also require that your business be at least two-years old before you can apply for business loans.

Smaller independent lenders (that are not affiliated with big banks) may view the Growth phase a little differently.

I personally work with several smaller lenders that will lump your business into the Growth phase if they see consistent profits over $10,000-$20,000 a month, even if your business is under two years old.

Either way, whether you're applying to a traditional big bank or a smaller non-bank lender, the key point is that you need to be able to show consistent financial growth, preferably in the five-figure range.

Can you get a cash loan in your company name if your 26-month-old business is bringing in $5,600 a month. Yes. But you'll likely qualify for under $10,000. And depending on the situation, it could be well under $5,000.

In the Growth phase, it's not just the length of time you've been in business. The amount of money your business brings in is possibly the biggest deciding factor for how much you can actually get in cash funding.

To put it all in perspective, if your Growth phase business is earning less than $5,000 a month, you may have an easier time just obtaining a few new business credit cards. But if you need cash, and your revenue is under $5,000 a month, you must keep your expectations fair.

Mature Phase

A mature business has many advantages -- and by mature, I mean five or more years old.

At this stage you probably have some well-seasoned business credit within your profile. You may have gone through a business loan or two or more. Positive cash flow should be consistent. You may be looking to expand geographically or into new markets.

Business funding is easier to obtain at this stage because companies at this level tend to be in a good financial flow. If your business revenue is good, it's not a matter of if you receive funding, but how much and from who.

Business lenders will be looking for solid financial statements at this stage. If you're looking to expand into new markets, you should have a business plan to get you from M to Z.

You'll likely be able to get funding from your existing business bank. Or (and this is what I frequently recommend) you may opt for something like a low-interest SBA loan.

Decline Phase

These are businesses typically within the 15–20 year old range. Not to say that all 15 year old businesses are in the decline phase. Yours might be going stronger than ever at the 20 year mark... and if so, kudos and high fives to you!

While older, established businesses have the longevity advantage going for them, their age may also point to stagnation. In 20 years, your customer base may be very different than when you first started out.

Think about how Wal-Mart demolished K-Mart. Look at how bigger department stores, like Sears and JCPenney, are slowly withering away.

Heck, the whole mall concept is under the guillotine. Fast fashion giants in China, like Shein, are quietly demolishing the American shopping experience. And let's not even talk about what Amazon has done to brick-and-mortar Main Street.

With all of that said, older businesses can be seen as risky investments to business lenders -- especially if you're in an industry that isn't as sexy as it was in yester-years.

Financial statements should show consistently inclining cash flow. Anything pointing to an ongoing downward trend is going to put you in a similar position as someone in the startup phase.

I imagine that most people reading this book aren't in the Decline phase yet. It's still good to know what to expect as your business continues to age.

You understand how your industry plays into the funding process... you understand how your revenue plays into it... and you know how the age of your business makes loan options possible, when combined with those other key points.

This is foundationally how lenders view your business, but we're not done yet. There are still some other key points to explore.

Think like a lender when looking at collateral

In the *Think like a lender when explaining your funding needs* section, I mentioned that lenders may view your equipment and property as assets.

This is important because these types of *long-term fixed assets* (and by *long-term fixed assets*, I mean property that won't be converted into cash within the next 12 months) may be viewed as collateral when applying for a business loan.

Now before we get too deep into this, it's only fair to mention that not every business lender is going to make collateral a priority, or even an option.

In situations where lenders are open to collateral, real estate tends to be the most requested item. And even then, it may only open doors if you currently have at least 40%-50% equity in the property, and the property is not located in a rural area.

Gianna came to me with a little less than 20% equity in a $500,000 Miami-based property, and I still could not get her approved for a $50,000 business loan, with the home as collateral.

Just to give you some reference on that entire situation, Gianna only got approved for a $7,000 business loan, which was about half of her monthly cash flow. Her personal credit was around 630-ish and she'd been in business for 18 months. Had her personal credit been stronger, she could have gotten a higher business loan.

So yes, lenders can be very picky!

What makes collateral desirable?

I find that businesses in the Growth and Mature phase tend to be the most likely to have collateral. They've usually built up their property and equipment investments at this stage.

In any case, if a lender asks for collateral outside of real estate, that item is likely going to be judged on seven factors:

1. **Marketability:** Is there an active secondary market where the item can be sold? Is there an auction or a website where these items are sold?

2. **Ascertainability:** Is it easy to gauge the value of the item? Unless you've got the recipe for Coca-Cola, which is a tremendous trade secret, it's easier to gauge the value of a physical item versus intellectual property.

3. **Stability:** Is the price of the item likely to remain stable? Does the item get updated so frequently that an older item loses significant value?

4. **Transferability:** Is ownership of the item easy to transfer? For example, it's a cinch to transfer the title of a vehicle from one owner to another. Transferability should be relatively fluid.

5. **Durability:** Is the item going to last for the lifetime of the loan and beyond?

6. **Absence of Liability:** Is the item easy to maintain? For example, there are plenty of car mechanics, but far fewer repair people for something like a Risograph machine.

7. **Equity:** How much ownership do you have over the item? My client had less than 20% equity in the home she wanted to put up for collateral. It wasn't enough for the lender. Every lender has their own underwriting guidelines, but I find that a minimum of 50% equity is usually the sweet spot.

As a sidenote, if you're getting an equipment loan, the lender may use the item you're purchasing as collateral. This is true for construction equipment, printing equipment and certain types of manufacturing equipment.

Either way, the lender will still use certain factors to decide if the item is worth it.

Think like a lender when laying the foundation for your business credit profile

Before we get into the nitty gritty of how lenders view your business credit profile, let's talk about a very important piece of the credit profile puzzle -- namely, the Small Business Financial Exchange (otherwise known as the SBFE).

The SBFE is a data exchange exclusively for small business creditors and lenders.

Each month, lending members provide information about businesses that get credit and cash funding from them. For example, if you have a Chase Ink business card, Chase reports details about your account to the SBFE database.

Since it's a data exchange, this also means SBFE members can view information about funding that businesses are receiving. So, not only does Chase provide details about your account to the SBFE for other members to see... Chase can also see details about the Bank of America business card you have.

Members of the SBFE have access to an extraordinary amount of information about your business including:

- ⊙ Your company name
- ⊙ Company address
- ⊙ DUNS number
- ⊙ EIN
- ⊙ NAICS code
- ⊙ Business credit card payment history (including your utilization)
- ⊙ Business line of credit, lease, and loan payment history

All the top business credit card issuers are members of the SBFE, including:

- ⊙ Chase
- ⊙ Citi
- ⊙ Bank of America
- ⊙ American Express
- ⊙ PNC
- ⊙ U.S. Bank
- ⊙ Capital One
- ⊙ Wells Fargo

⊙ Plus 130+ more financial institutions, credit unions and alternative lenders. (You can call your bank to ask if they're members of the SBFE.)

The SBFE also has a limited number of Certified Vendors. They are LexisNexis, Dun & Bradstreet, Experian and Equifax.

These Certified Vendors collect raw data from the SBFE, and then turn it into risk products specifically for other SBFE members. That data also gets used to create business credit scores, credit reports, and other risk analysis products.

This is quoted directly from the SBFE website:

"Vendors receive your account information from the SBFE Data Warehouse™ and combine it with other data sources (examples: public record, Secretary of State filings, and trade-type account receivable data) on your company. Certified Vendors compile this information to create a credit report and credit risk score on your business."

And just to further clarify, not every business credit card or loan that's reported to the SBFE is going to show up on your business credit reports.

Here's what the SBFE says about that:

"....the payment history reported by SBFE members will only be found in a subset of credit risk products developed by D&B, Experian, Equifax and LexisNexis Risk Solutions. Each commercial credit reporting agency offers various types of credit reports and scores that are built from different data sources (which may or may not include SBFE data)."

In a nutshell, if you want credit or a loan from a lender in the SBFE, there's a very strong chance they're going to check your company through a proprietary SBFE report. Remember, lenders can give information about you... but they can also receive it.

How to maximize your SBFE profile so you can get high credit limits

Let's say you have an American Express business card with a $5,000 limit, and a $4,700 balance. You've been paying that balance down, but it's still high.

Your goal is to get a Chase Ink Business card. And of course, you want the highest limits possible because you're a Funding Prepper.

But, before you apply for anything -- be it a credit card, a loan, or a line of credit -- you should always understand what factors will cause the bank to approve/deny you. You'll head to LocateYourLender.com for that info.

LocateYourLender.com will tell you that Chase checks your personal credit, even when you apply for a business card. (As most business credit card issuers do.) They'll run your Experian FICO 8 credit score.

In addition, they'll check the SBFE, your Experian Business report, your Equifax Business report and possibly your Dun & Bradstreet report (all of which I'll talk about in the next section).

Even though American Express doesn't show up anywhere on your personal or business credit reports -- (unless you default) -- when Chase checks the SBFE, they'll still be able to see that you've got a $5,000 limit with a $4,700 balance on your American Express business card.

Okay so, knowing all that background knowledge, how do you think your starting limit is going to be affected if you were to apply for that Chase Ink business card right now?

If you said, "*My limits could be hindered*," then you're correct.

Even though the American Express card isn't reporting to any of your business or personal credit reports, it's still holding court at the SBFE. That high balance is definitely going to weigh into whether

Chase accepts or denies your Ink business card application, as well as what you receive as the starting limit.

Besides that, because your Amex card has a balance that's close to the limit, it's possible that high utilization is reflected in your business credit scores, which in turn could negatively affect limits and terms you get from other lenders.

The big takeaway... just because something is hidden, and we don't have access to it, doesn't mean it's not affecting your credit profile.

If you're going to seek out additional business credit or loans, you need to make sure that the balances on your existing business cards are low. You don't want to be near the limit because that's going to affect your approval rates and starting limits on other business products.

And if possible, pay your bill as soon as the statement comes out. You want to establish and maintain a payment history that makes SBFE members say yes without hesitation. You want to be able to glide through those automated applications without getting any, "*You're application is under review*" notifications.

If it shows that you pay your bills quickly, and you keep your balances low, you're more likely to receive high limits.

Beyond the SBFE: The three main business credit reports guiding lender's decisions

Just like consumer lenders look at your personal credit reports, business lenders utilize business credit reports to determine how risky it is to give cash or credit to your company.

But that's where the differences end. Business credit reports contain tradeline payment history, but they also incorporate a lot of publicly available data about your company that can make or break your funding approvals. Think of them as a mix of both credit and consumer reports.

EXPERIAN BUSINESS

The Experian Business credit report includes information about:

- ⊙ Active accounts,

- ⊙ New accounts you've opened,

- ⊙ The highest/lowest 6-month balance,

- ⊙ Total balance of your tradelines,

- ⊙ DBT (Days Beyond Terms).

In addition to collecting data from your lenders and suppliers, Experian also builds your business credit file from court records, as well as state filing offices, credit card companies, marketing databases, collection agencies, and a variety of other public sources.

If you have any business registrations, liens, judgments, bankruptcies or Uniform Commercial Code (UCC) filings against your business, those are on your Experian Business report as well.

EQUIFAX BUSINESS

The Equifax Business credit report lists slightly different information than Experian.

Equifax includes:

- ⊙ The number of tradelines you have, both open and closed, including those that have been charged off,

- ⊙ Highest amount owed on business credit cards,

- ⊙ Delinquent accounts, including the total past due.

Like Experian, the Equifax report contains information from public databases about business judgments, liens, UCCs, and bankruptcies.

DUN & BRADSTREET

Dun & Bradstreet business credit reports are the most comprehensive out of these top 3. They contain:

- ⊙ A complete company profile, including annual sales, number of employees, business age and principal managers/owners.

- ⊙ All the business tradelines you have.

- ⊙ How much credit you've been granted.

- ⊙ Past due amounts.

- ⊙ How many times you've been late making payments.

- ⊙ The Legal Events section shows liens, UCC filings, bankruptcies, lawsuits and judgements.

- ⊙ The Risk Assessment section features all your Dun & Bradstreet ratings (basically like credit scores), as well as the recommended maximum amount they suggest creditors give you.

Depending on your industry, there may be other business credit bureaus out there. For example, if you have a trucking or a construction business, then you're probably familiar with Ansonia -- which is an Equifax company. If you're in the seafood industry, then you might know about Seafax.

These are just the most widely used across the board for general funding purposes.

How long does derogatory information stay on your business credit reports?

Business credit reports aren't regulated by the federal government like their personal counterparts. There are no set rules for how long an account can stay on your business credit report, be it good or bad. Each bureau seems to set their own rules.

However, after a bit of digging, I found that Experian Business does provide timestamps for the data on their business reports:

- ⊙ Trade data is reported for: 36 months
- ⊙ Bankruptcies: 9 years and 9 months
- ⊙ Judgments: 6 years and 9 months
- ⊙ Tax liens: 6 years and 9 months
- ⊙ Uniform Commercial Code filings: 5 years
- ⊙ Collections: 6 years and 9 months
- ⊙ Bank, government and leasing data: 36 months

Unfortunately, Equifax nor Dun & Bradstreet provide specific account retention information, like Experian does.

Think like a lender when looking at your business credit scores

Each of your business credit reports includes a credit score, and those scores can determine:

- ⊙ Whether you get approved or denied for credit, loans, lines of credit or leasing,
- ⊙ Funding limits (which is how much you're approved for),
- ⊙ Funding terms (whether it's the favorable net 30 or a term between 2-4 years),
- ⊙ And how high or low your business insurance premiums are.

As you've already read, the business credit bureaus all report different data. This means your scores are calculated differently at each bureau. (FICO doesn't rule the roost over here like they do with your personal credit scores.)

Because there are so many different factors at work, it's a bit more challenging to raise your business credit scores. Challenging, but not impossible.

To do this effectively, we have to look at the constant across all three bureaus. Besides the publicly available information about your company, the one constant is your tradelines.

Remember, a *tradeline* is basically an account like a credit card account, a loan account or a line of credit. In business credit land, there are two types of credit tradelines.

A *vendor tradeline* is like a retail credit card. It's credit that has been extended to you from a specific company. For example, Uline may provide you with a net 30 vendor tradeline, which means you have 30 days to pay an invoice on any products ordered from their catalog.

Financial tradelines are credit card accounts, loan accounts and so on. A Visa or Mastercard account that appears on your business credit report would be a financial tradeline.

Your business credit scores incorporate data from both vendor and financial tradelines, however not all vendors or financial institutions report to all the business credit bureaus.

Trust me, I'm not talking in circles! I'll cover all of this in the Pinnacle Score Pathway, a little later.

Just know that *the way* you pay your tradelines is more important than anything else. It's great to pay your tradelines on time when you're talking about personal credit. But I'll be giving you some slightly different suggestions for your business tradelines. That's because the same things that matter on your personal credit, matter 10x more on your business credit.

Businesses spend more money than consumers. As a result, business creditors and lenders tend to give more money than their personal counterparts. You want to understand the rules, play by the rules, and meticulously dot your I's and cross your t's to make your business credit scores strong.

> *Reader question: I was able to get a business credit card without having a business credit score. Do business credit scores really affect your ability to get business funding?*

It is very much possible to get business credit cards without business credit scores.

I got my first American Express business card without any business credit scores. (But I did have personal American Express cards.) Even with my own success, I still strongly advocate that it's better to apply with scores than without.

And yes, this is especially true if you're looking to get a business loan. Business credit scores can make-or-break a hard money deal. The more money you're asking for, the more those scores matter.

There are four business credit scores that you should be aware of. Depending on your industry, you might find more than these four. For the sake of commonality, these are the ones that affect nearly all businesses.

You'll be able to gain access to any of these scores through Nav.com. The $49.95 a month Nav Prime account includes access to the Dun & Bradstreet, Experian and Equifax business credit reports and their associated business credit scores. For an extra fee, they also provide the SBSS score which is used to pre-screen you for the SBA 7(a) loan, Community Advantage loans, and Express Bridge Loans.

Besides reports and scores, they provide a Nav checking account and a Nav business credit building card that has no credit check or security deposit required. (They will connect to your bank account via Plaid to set a limit on the card.)

At the time I'm writing this book, there are no other websites that provide business credit reports and scores like Nav.com. Makes the choice to subscribe pretty easy!

Dun & Bradstreet PAYDEX

The PAYDEX score was designed to show lenders how quickly you pay your business bills. It's one of the most widely monitored scores for business lending purposes, and it is available at Nav.com.

According to Dun & Bradstreet, *"The PAYDEX Score is a dollar-weighted indicator intended to reflect a business's past payment performance."*

When they say *dollar weighted,* they mean larger debts hold more point boosting power than smaller ones. A $15,000 invoice payment is going to affect your PAYDEX score more positively than a $200 payment.

You're also scored based on payment data Dun & Bradstreet receives from suppliers and vendors. Your score will vary depending on if you make early payments, on-time payments, late payments, or if an account has been sent to collections.

The PAYDEX score itself ranges between 0-100. The higher the PAYDEX, the less likely you are to default on your payments, and the more likely lenders are to give you larger limits.

So how do you score as close to 100 as possible?

This is where *the way* you make your payments comes into play. You'll need to pay your business invoices *30 days earlier* than the due date. If you do that consistently, you'll score a perfect 100.

A score of 90 means you pay your invoices 20 days before they're due. An 80 means that you're paying those invoices on time. Scores between 70-79 show that you pay your invoices 15 days beyond the term. 50 or below means you're making payment 30+ days beyond the invoice term.

FYI, if you're not in the 90-100 range, you're doing it all wrong. But if you'd like to give yourself a little grace, I'd say that it's perfectly fine to aim for a solid 90.

In fact, you may notice that when you pay certain invoices 30 days early, they'll get marked as a *cash payment* on your Dun & Bradstreet report. This isn't necessarily a bad thing. But I prefer to see an account marked as credit rather than cash. This means, my personal preference is to pay 20 days ahead of time.

How to get a PAYDEX score

You'll need a DUNS number, as well as a minimum of three payments from three different suppliers. And when I say three different suppliers, all of them must report to Dun & Bradstreet for those payments to count towards your PAYDEX score.

You can get a DUNS number for free on the Dun & Bradstreet website. It can take up to 30 days to get the number this way.

If you prefer, you can get an expedited DUNS number within 8 business days for $229 (at the time I'm writing this). You can find links for both regular and expedited at FundingPreppers.com/BookLinks

Once you get the DUNS number, you'll have a basic Dun & Bradstreet credit file created for your business, as well as a company profile on the Dun & Bradstreet business directory.

I strongly suggest completing the company profile. This information is often used by other business directories, so you'll want to make sure it's all accurate and correct. They're going to ask you for:

- ⊙ Legal name of your business
- ⊙ Business address
- ⊙ Business phone number
- ⊙ Name of the business owner, president, or CEO
- ⊙ Legal structure of the business (Partnership, LLC, S-Corp, C-Corp)
- ⊙ Year the business was created
- ⊙ Primary business industry
- ⊙ Total number of full- and part-time employees

If you haven't already, begin actively seeking opportunities to raise your PAYDEX score, since it's going to take at least a few months for a score to be generated.

Also keep in mind that your PAYDEX score (or other D&B scores) may be viewed if you're bidding on government/non-government contracts or trying to negotiate commercial space for your business. So again, the faster you set up your profile and generate a score, the better.

Additional Dun & Bradstreet scores

Dun & Bradstreet has four other scores that may be on a lender's radar.

D&B Rating

Measures your company's financial strength, based on your company age, size, industry and financial statements. This rating tells lenders how creditworthy your business is.

If you're bidding on government contracts or negotiating payment terms with suppliers, you'll want to keep your D&B Rating high. This is a vital number in the government contract universe.

The D&B Rating is broken down by Rating Classification and the Composite Credit Appraisal.

The Rating Classification is assigned to you when you provide Dun & Bradstreet with your company's most recent financial statements. If you don't provide your financial statements, you don't get a Rating Classification, so not providing your financial statements does affect the overall D&B Rating.

The Composite Credit Appraisal is based on your company's payment history, years in business, public records, financial records and other factors.

How would a lender use the D&B Rating?

Experienced lenders use a variety of tools when assessing a business loan application. The D&B Rating would be just one piece of the puzzle.

A lender might incorporate the D&B Rating into the automated approval process. It may be used to gauge how your company's financial growth compares to other similarly sized businesses in your industry, as part of their risk assessment. They may use it to see how creditworthy the business is, based on how they pay their debts.

How to increase your D&B Rating

You can't change certain things like your industry, company age or the number of employees you have. However, for the sake of getting a complete D&B Rating, you'll need to submit current business financial statements to your Dun & Bradstreet profile on a regular basis. And as always with Dun & Bradstreet, paying your business debts early should be a priority.

Viability Rating

The Viability Rating measures your company's current and future health to predict how likely you are to go out of business or file for bankruptcy within the next 12 months, as compared to all companies in the Dun & Bradstreet database.

How would a lender use the Viability Rating?

Before deep diving into your application, a lender might view your D&B profile as a first-pass filter.

They may look at your Viability Rating first. The score itself ranges between 1 and 9, with 1 being the least risky and 9 being the highest risk. Yours is a 7, which is pretty steep.

At this point, the lender will look at other compensating factors in the application, like personal credit scores, financial statements, a business plan, and so on.

If the lender decides the loan is workable, they may give you a higher interest rate or shorter repayment terms because of your high Viability Rating.

How to increase your Viability Rating

Because you're being compared to all companies in the D&B database (or all companies within a specific segment), there are certain factors you cannot control. For instance, you can't control the number of years you've been in business, the number of employees you have, your industry, or the geographic location of the business.

You can, however, control your tradelines and how you pay them. Having 4+ tradelines reporting to Dun & Bradstreet is optimal. Paying your tradelines early (before net 30) keeps you in the safe zone.

Adding your company financial statements to your Dun & Bradstreet account seems to help, since your company is being compared to millions of others. The more well-rounded your company profile is, the better.

Failure Score

The Failure Score predicts how likely your company is to go bankrupt or cease operations without paying your creditors, within the next 12 months.

The score is based on several factors including, vendor payment data, the type of business you're in (if you're in a risky industry, this is where is starts becoming problematic), the age and net worth of the business, if you have any public filings like lawsuits, liens or judgements. These elements are weighed against other companies in your industry to come up with the Failure Score.

How would a lender use the Failure Score?

Failure Scores range from 1,001-1,875, with 1,001 being the highest risk of failure, and 1,875 being the lowest probability of failure. As with most of these predictive scores, each lender will have their own approval range.

If you have a Failure Score ranging between 1,001-1,339, you're technically not in a position to receive any kind of funding. If you do, expect the interest rate to be downright disrespectful. At that point, you should be figuring out how to get up to at least 1,510.

How to increase your Failure Score

Your Failure Score is one of those metrics that tends to increase as your business ages, and as vendors/suppliers continue adding payment data to your D&B Report. The main thing you can do is continue paying your business bills early and steer clear of situations that could cause the business legal trouble.

Delinquency Predictor Score

The Delinquency Predictor Score gauges how likely your company is to fall behind on your bills, file for bankruptcy, or go out of business in the next 12 months. In the personal credit realm, a delinquency is a tradeline that is 30-90 days late. However, D&B defines a severely delinquent company, *"as a business with at least 10% of its dollars more than 90 days past due."*

The score is primarily built from your payment history with vendors/suppliers who report to D&B, in addition to financial statements (that you submit to your D&B profile), and public records such as liens, judgements and lawsuits.

How would a lender use the Delinquency Predictor Score?

The score ranges from 101-670. A score of 101 means your company has the highest risk of severe delinquency. 670 means you're not likely to pay your bills late.

Prime lenders who use it may not approve anyone with a Delinquency Predictor Score of 101-480. Alternative lenders may range from 453-579.

How to increase your Delinquency Predictor Score?

D&B says the Delinquency Predictor Score is recalculated whenever they collect a new relevant piece of information about the company. This means, the longer your company is in the D&B database, and the more business bills you pay early, the higher your Delinquency Predictor Score.

Experian Business - Intelliscore Plus V2

The Experian Business Intelliscore shows lenders how likely your business is to default on a payment within the next 12 months.

It's built from both your Experian personal credit data as well as your business credit data. This means if you've got bad personal credit, it's going to follow you over here to the business side. But if you have fair personal credit (no derogatory accounts, but high utilization) you can still get a pretty good Intelliscore.

The total score is comprised of five main factors:

- ⊙ 50% of the score is based on past due accounts,
- ⊙ 15% is based on public records and legal claims against your business,
- ⊙ 15% is based on your utilization. This is how much debt you have as compared to your credit limits,
- ⊙ 10% is based on your payments and how quickly you make them,
- ⊙ 10% is based on how long you've been in business, your industry and the size of your business.

When you look at your Intelliscore report, you'll see these metrics expressed in different sections.

- ⊙ The *Days Beyond Terms (DBT)* section indicates how many days it takes for you to pay your invoices. If you see a 0 in this section, it means you pay your invoices right on time.

- The *Summary of Tradelines* shows which vendors and suppliers report your payments to Experian Business.

- There's also a section for legal filings against your business including judgements, liens, UCC filings, and bankruptcy.

Intelliscore V2 ranges between 1-100. The closer you are to 100, the less risky you appear to lenders. Anything over 75 means you're in a pretty good position to receive funding. Between 51-74 is good, but you may not get the instant approval of having a score over 75.

A score between 26-50 is considered fair. You will not qualify for all forms of funding. Depending on what's happening with the rest of your credit, you may only qualify for sub-prime options. And if your score is under 25, you WILL NOT get approved for traditional business loans. This is where you get asset-based funding options like merchant cash advances.

How to get an Intelliscore

You only need one account reporting to Experian Business to get an Intelliscore.

Equifax Business Delinquency Score

The Equifax Business Delinquency Score predicts the likelihood of a business becoming severely delinquent on vendor tradelines within a 12 month time frame.

Like Experian's Intelliscore, Equifax's Delinquency Score is built from both personal and vendor credit data, as well as public records, and information from the SBFE.

This score ranges from 397-695. A Business Delinquency Score of 0 indicates bankruptcy.

According to Equifax, a lower score indicates a higher probability of severe delinquency, while a higher score shows a lower chance of delinquency. (In other words, Low Score = High Risk whereas High Score = Low Risk.)

You only need one business tradeline reporting to get a Business Delinquency Score. However, I can tell you that even with an Equifax FICO 8 credit score of 720 or more, your Business Delinquency Score will still be poor if you only have 1 business tradeline reporting.

How to get an Equifax Business Delinquency Score

My professional observation is that you need to have at least three or more business tradelines reporting to Equifax to really see a boost on your score.

FICO Small Business Scoring Service (SBSS)

This one isn't as popular as the three previously mentioned scores, but if you're applying for a Small Business Administration (SBA) loan or line of credit, it is THE score you need to pay attention to.

This score ranges between 0-300. According to Nav.com, it's built from four different factors.

They are:

- ◉ Consumer credit reports for the principals/guarantors of the business (up to five owners),
- ◉ Business credit reports for the business,
- ◉ Application data supplied on the loan application,
- ◉ Business financial data.

The most important factor here being the owner's personal credit. So once again, if you have shaky personal credit, you will unfortunately feel the backlash. Depending on what kinds of derogatory accounts you have on your credit, it could take years before you attain a decent SBSS score.

SBA lenders use the SBSS to pre-screen applicants for 7(a) loans, if the loan is under $1 million dollars. For 7(a) loans, your SBSS score should be at least 155-160. I personally recommend Funding Preppers come in with at least 165-175, to account for changing economic conditions.

(In case you're not familiar, 7(a) loans can be used for working capital, inventory, equipment, real estate, business acquisition or refinancing business debt. If your business is over 2 years old, and you've maintained a strong financial profile, this is the loan I almost always recommend.)

SBA-backed lenders also use the SBSS score for the Community Advantage loan, where you'll need to have at least a 140, and the Express Bridge Loan, which requires a 130.

Outside of the SBA, over 7,500 banks, credit card issuers and alternative lenders make business lending decisions with the SBSS score. Each lender has their own minimum, but I advise Funding Preppers to look at the SBA cutoff score of 160 as the lowest to go. Traditional banks tend to have higher requirements than the SBA. For example, if you need funding to buy a franchise, you'll need to come in the door with an SBSS score of at least 190-200.

Ansonia Risk Score

Over the years, I've dealt with several business owners in the trucking industry, so I figured I'd include the Ansonia Risk Score.

Carriers (truckers and trucking companies) use the Ansonia Risk Score to see how risky it is to work with specific brokers. Brokers build up their Ansonia Risk Score to get credit from truck drivers. Without the truck drivers, a broker cannot run their business.

For example, if I'm a truck driver and Lincoln Brokerage has a load available from Delaware to Texas, I'll look up Lincoln's Ansonia Risk Score to see how diligent they are about paying vendors.

This score ranges between 0-100. Lincoln Brokerage is showing a Risk Score of 87, which means they're relatively low risk. If Lincoln's score was below 69, I wouldn't want to carry the load. There would be a strong possibility that I wouldn't get paid.

To get a Risk Score, at least two suppliers must report their payment history over a three-month period. By the 4th month, a score will be generated.

Ansonia Credit Data is an Equifax company. While I'm not 100% sure that data from Ansonia affects your Equifax Business score, I wouldn't doubt that it could.

TransCredit

TransCredit is like Ansonia in that they both provide risk analysis for brokers in the transportation industry. However, Ansonia provides a Risk Score, whereas TransCredit provides the Transportation Credit Score, as well as credit reports for shippers, brokers and carriers.

One of the most valuable parts of their credit report is the Days-to-Pay section. Any company that wants to do business with you can see how long it takes you to pay your vendors. Obviously, paying your vendors on time is an absolute must to maintain a good score.

Scores range from 0-100. A score between 1-59 shows that you're an extreme risk. At 60-75, you're considered a high risk, and from 76-89, you're a moderate risk. Anything above 90 shows you have a low risk of paying vendors late.

The Transportation Credit Score is automatically going to be a zero, if you're a brand-new broker. However, you do have the ability to manually add your own credit references to the credit report. For instance, if you've already worked with a carrier, you may add the company as a credit reference.

TransCredit manually verifies each account you add, which means your credit score won't be updated overnight. But this process is a lot faster than waiting the 3-6 months it normally takes carriers to provide this information on their own.

Think like a lender when building your business credit scores

Now that you know about the four main business credit scores, and you understand the importance of each one, let's work on building or improving those scores.

The logic here is that the better your business credit scores, the higher your starting limits on business credit cards, and the bigger your loan offers.

This means if you want the best funding terms, it's better to NOT use business credit cards as the basis for building your business credit scores. And it's not because you can't get business credit cards without business scores.

I mentioned before that banks will give you business credit cards, even if you don't have business scores. I just know that if you wait until you have nice business scores, you tend to get higher credit limits.

And if you already have some business cards, that's fine. These steps will simply help you to get more significant credit limit increases over time.

The Pinnacle Score Pathway

I use the Pinnacle Score Pathway with my Funding Prepper clients because it doesn't matter if your business is brand new or seasoned with seven years of history. You can implement this strategy with good personal credit or bad. Just keep in mind that Experian, Equifax and the FICO SBSS all incorporate your personal credit scores into the formulation of your business scores.

So even though the Pinnacle Score Pathway works for all credit levels, you're going to see the best possible scores if your personal credit doesn't have any derogatory accounts, and your FICO 8 is above 700.

Even if your personal credit isn't great, you can still get decent business credit scores at Experian and Equifax. But it's not going to be as momentous as someone who has 700+ FICO 8 scores. Keep your expectations reasonable.

And in case you're wondering, yes... it is going to cost you some money on the front end. You can't build business credit history if you're not presently spending money. But the result of this modest investment will be a bulletproof business credit profile. Boom!

1). You'll need a minimum of five tradelines reporting positive payment history on each of your business credit reports (including the SBFE), for at least 3-6 months.

As you've already learned, each credit bureau says they need a certain number of tradelines reporting before a score is generated. For Dun & Bradstreet, it's three. And for Experian and Equifax, it's one.

However, just because you have the minimum number of tradelines reporting doesn't mean you're automatically going to get the best scores possible.

The Equifax Business score is built from both your personal and business credit data. Even when I had a 720+ FICO 8 score, and the one tradeline needed to generate a score, my Equifax Business score never got past 375. And that's not good! 375 is the equivalent of having bad business credit.

To put this in a better perspective, I never paid any of my accounts late. I had no derogatory accounts on either my personal or business credit. Utilization was modest on my personal accounts... certainly well below the 30% that FICO recommends.

This is a clear indication that a single tradeline may be enough to get a score, but it's rarely enough to generate a score that gets you well-funded.

Having five tradelines with a good payment history over six months shows that you can handle debt. This is what lenders and creditors in the business space are looking for. They want to see that you've got skin in the game.

So how do you do this?

2). Establish at least one secured financial tradeline. Have you ever heard of a secured credit card? You deposit $500 into a savings account, and the bank gives you a Visa or Mastercard with a $500 limit. The credit limit is secured by your deposit.

Secured cards are great if you have bad credit because you're not applying on the merit of your credit score. Provided you have the security deposit, you're usually good to go.

While there are several secured credit cards for personal use, there are only a couple for business purposes.

And if you find yourself scrolling Google for a few more, always make sure that you're looking for *secured business cards*, and that each of the cards offered are genuine business credit cards. Sometimes websites will list personal secured cards as business cards because they want you to apply.

In the meantime, if I find additional secured business cards after this book is published, you'll find direct links to them at (FundingPreppers.com/BookLinks).

The Bank of America Business Advantage Unlimited Cash Rewards Secured Card reports to the SBFE, but does not show up on any of your business credit reports.

I know what some of you are thinking... especially those of you who know a little something about business credit. Why on earth would you want a business credit card that doesn't report to any of your business credit reports???

Quite simply, because if it's reporting to the SBFE, it's going to affect your entire business credit profile.

Remember, Dun & Bradstreet, Equifax Business and Experian Business are Certified Vendors that use data from accounts being reported on the SBFE. Your business credit scores and any credit limits you receive are swayed because of the data being reported to the SBFE, even if that data doesn't appear on any of your credit reports.

Let's break down the 'why' behind all of this.

If you apply for a personal credit card, and it's denied, the bank must inform you of the reason(s) why you weren't approved... the credit bureau they used... and the score that was used to make the decision. It's called an *adverse action letter*, and it's a governmental regulation that a lender provides it to applicants that get denied.

Business credit, however, doesn't have the same regulations. If you apply for a business credit card or a loan using your EIN, a lender must tell you that you've been declined. They can inform you of this in writing or verbally.

However, they don't have to give you a list of reasons why you were declined. Nor do they have to tell you if and which credit score they used. The best you can do is contact the lender and request a list of reasons why you were declined.

(This is all outlined in the Equal Credit Opportunity Act, otherwise known as Regulation B.)

When you understand it from this perspective, then you can see how decisions are made from data you can see, as well as the hidden data that doesn't look like it's being reported.

This is why it's vital to cover all your bases when it comes to your business credit. You can't think like a consumer lender when you're applying for business credit.

Whew! With that said, let's circle back around to the Bank of America Business Advantage Unlimited Cash Rewards Secured Card. This card requires a deposit between $1,000-$50,000, and your credit limit will be equal to your deposit.

If you use the card regularly, and pay it in full every month, there's a chance Bank of America will make the card unsecured, and they'll refund your deposit.

Next up is the First National Bank of Omaha (FNBO) Business Edition Secured Mastercard. This card reports to all three personal credit bureaus (Experian, Equifax and Transunion), as well as Dun & Bradstreet and Experian Business.

You may deposit $2,200-$110,000, and your credit limit will be 110% of the security deposit. Even though the card will never become unsecured, they are granting you a little extra spending money with that 110% limit.

One thing to keep in mind about FNBO is that they do not allow you to have multiple versions of their card. So, you can have one personal card, and one business card. If you attempt to get more than one FNBO-backed business credit cards, they'll shut down subsequent accounts.

And finally, let's talk about the Credit Strong Business Credit Builder Account. This one isn't a secured credit card. It's actually a secured loan. I like to think of it as a reverse loan.

You'll pay into the account for 25 months, and then you receive the money once it's paid off. As you're making payments, they get reported to Equifax Business, the SBFE and PayNet. According to the Credit Strong website, they'll soon be reporting to Experian Business and Dun & Bradstreet, but they're not providing a firm date.

You can choose between a loan amount of $2,500, $5,000, $10,000 or $25,000. Each loan amount requires a one-time fee. If you pay a higher one-time fee of $349-$749, the interest on the loan will be 0%, and the monthly payments will be lower. Or you can provide a smaller one-time fee of $149-$499, and have higher monthly payments because of the added interest.

3). Set up 2+ vendor tradelines. You may also see vendor tradelines referred to as *vendor credit, supplier credit* or *net 30 accounts* because of the terms of payment -- you have 30 days to pay the invoice in full.

Used properly, vendor tradelines are an excellent way to increase your business credit scores, as well as to improve cash flow if you're selling or using the items before the invoice is due.

For example, if you're buying from Judy's Sock Company, and selling those socks on your website before the net 30 invoice is due, your cash flow is no longer tied up in inventory. Business lenders love to see productive moves like this.

One of my favorite vendor tradelines is the Nav Prime account available through Nav.com. (Remember, Nav.com is the company that provides the top business credit reports and scores.)

You simply set up an account with Nav in your business name and make your regular monthly/quarterly payments. Those payments automatically get reported to Dun & Bradstreet, Experian Business and Equifax Business.

If you don't have any business credit, I strongly recommend setting up Nav first. It's inexpensive... it allows you to get your

Experian Business and Equifax Business scores rolling... it provides a product you're going to need anyway... and most important, it's going to be a stepping-stone to additional funding opportunities.

My second recommendation – Shogun Roasting – is another easy-to-obtain vendor tradeline. This is a coffee vendor that carries standard grind, espresso grind and whole bean blends. They report to Dun & Bradstreet, Experian Business, Equifax Business and Creditsafe.

Before applying, you must have been in business for at least three-months, and you'll need to place one order with Shogun before you can apply for a vendor tradeline. After your first order, they'll give you a net 30 or net 60 account, with a $400-$1,000 limit – depending on your Experian Business score. If you don't have an Experian Business score, you're still eligible for a net 30 account, with a $400 limit.

Third on the list is Uline. Uline provides boxes, tape and other assorted shipping/packing supplies, janitorial goods, safety products, and office furniture. They report to Dun & Bradstreet and Experian Business.

If your business is 6+ months old, and you've got at least Nav and Shogun Roasting reporting on your business credit, they are more likely to automatically provide net 30 terms.

How does automatic approval work at Uline? Sometimes when you've placed items in your cart, and you get to the payment page, they'll offer you net 30 terms without you doing anything. I find this to be true if your order is above $150. Even if you're not automatically approved, you can still apply for a net 30 account on the website.

Moving on, if your business needs industrial maintenance supplies, janitorial products, office/hospitality furniture, restaurant supplies, warehouse goods, or even lab equipment, then #4 on the list – Grainger -- is going to be the tradeline for you.

Grainger reports to Dun & Bradstreet and Equifax. Your business should be at least three months old, and I suggest at least one additional tradeline on your Equifax Business Credit. (Now you see why Nav is so vital!)

You'll need to set up a customer account at Grainger and then call their customer service to set up the credit line. They're going to review your business credit. If approved, the starting limit is $1,000, but if your business credit is already strong, you could get more.

Moving from industrial goods to web services takes us to #5 on the list, Creative Analytics. Creative Analytics is a digital marketing agency that specializes in web design, social media marketing and SEO. They report to Dun & Bradstreet, Equifax Business and Credit Safe.

Your business must be at least 30 days old before applying for a net 30 account. You must also have an EIN and DUNS number, as well as no derogatory account or delinquencies on your business credit report. Credit lines range from $1,000-$10,000.

Just so you have an idea of what's possible, if you order their $149 a month web design package, you'll get a $2,000 tradeline. And if you get the $449 a month web design/maintenance package, your tradeline will be $10,000.

CEO Creative is a less expensive option if you're looking for web services. They provide web and graphic design, print services, customizable products, office supplies, and electronics. And they report to Dun & Bradstreet, Equifax Business and Credit Safe.

To apply for the CEO Creative net 30 account, you must have been in business for at least 30 days with no derogatories or delinquencies on your business credit report. There's a $49 sign-up fee for the program, and you'll need to spend at least $40 a month. The minimum credit line you'll receive is $1,100.

Now, if you're looking for virtual office space, Opus provides a pretty good deal for tradeline building. The Opus Virtual Office (VO) is available at 650 locations and costs $99 a month.

The virtual service includes a local telephone number, a live receptionist to answer your calls during business hours, after-hours voicemail, a corporate mailing address and more. They start reporting to Dun & Bradstreet and Creditsafe after the first 30 days of service. However, you will have to specifically request that they report to the bureaus. They won't do it by default.

Alrighty! We are moving and grooving along with #8, which is Wise Business Plans. Although the name says, 'business plans,' they do provide other services like pitch deck creation, business formation, licensing assistance, website design, branding and digital marketing.

To get a net 30 account you'll need to be set up with the Secretary of State for at least 30 days, you'll need an EIN, and no derogatory accounts on your business credit report. Their lines of credit vary according to your business credit profile, and they report to Experian Business, Equifax Business and Creditsafe.

Number 9 on the list is the Brand Apparel Club. They provide custom and wholesale t-shirts and (as the name states) branded apparel. So, if you want a t-shirt or a sweatshirt with your company logo on it, this is the place to get it.

Before being granted net 30 status, you'll need to join the club for $69.99 a year. In addition, you'll need to order 12 items per design for custom printed or embroidered items, or a minimum of $250 for blank apparel and accessories.

Once those requirements are met, you'll be able to select net 30 as your payment choice whenever ordering. For the first 5 orders (at minimum), you'll need to pay 50% up front. If you pay those invoices early or on time, you'll get full net 30 access at the 5th order.

Brand Apparel Club reports to Equifax Business, Creditsafe, Ansonia and Cortera on the first week of every month.

Last on the list is The Red Spectrum, which will give you a boost on Equifax Business. They sell business eBooks, audiobooks, courses, coaching services, logos and other business-related services. Regardless of what you order, you'll receive a $3,500 tradeline on that first order.

They also offer a Business Builder account that solely provides a tradeline. There's a startup fee of $99, and then it's $54.95 a month. For $153.95, you get an initial tradeline of $3,500 reporting.

Each month that you continue subscribing, they raise that amount another $1,500. This means in month two you'll have $5,000 being reported, and in month three, it'll be $6,500.

On top of that, if you pay a one-time fee of $199-$999, they'll start your tradeline limit with an extra $3,500-$25,000. So, if you decide to take the initial $3,500 tradeline, and you add in the one-time payment of $199 for an extra $3,500, your initial payment will be $352.95, and you'll have a $7,000 tradeline. From there, every month it'll still go up another $1,500.

4). Purchase something every single month and pay off your tradelines as soon as you receive the invoice/statement. If you recall, your Dun & Bradstreet PAYDEX score is based on the number of vendors that report your tradelines and how soon you pay those invoices.

Therefore, if you're going to stay on the sunny side of the street, paying invoices early is better than paying on time. You should have no lates whatsoever.

Do inquiries on a business credit report cost points?

Dun & Bradstreet PAYDEX scores and Equifax Business scores are typically not affected by inquiries. However, inquiries can cause you to lose points on Experian Business and FICO SBSS scores.

Experian Business provides a list of factors they use to generate business scores, including:

- ⊙ Current collections, liens, judgments, bankruptcies or other derogatory public records on your business profile,

- ⊙ The status, recency, frequency and dollar amounts of any applicable liens, judgments or bankruptcies,

- ⊙ An increased trend in slow payment of obligations,

- ⊙ **An increase in the number of business credit inquiries or applications that are generated by the business or the owner, (There it is!)**

- ⊙ The number of trade experiences, balances outstanding, payment habits, credit utilization and trends over time,

- ⊙ Years in business, line of business or Standard Industrial Classification (SIC) code, size of business and other demographic data.

Yup, even business inquiries can zap you. And if you're curious to see how many points you'll potentially lose on an inquiry, check out Experian's Business Credit Score Planner. It's a quickie questionnaire that'll help you understand how the changes you make affect your business credit score. There's a direct link at (FundingPreppers.com/BookLinks).

What if one of these lenders/vendors declines my application?

There are usually two reasons why you'd be declined.

Number one, you're not following the steps in the Pinnacle Score Pathway. Maybe you're trying to get other tradelines or credit cards before you've had a chance to let your business credit foundation grow.

Whoa, whoa, whoa... slow down! Take some time to build a solid base, and then you'll be ready for everything else. The Pinnacle Score Pathway lays the essential groundwork. It gives you a sturdy foundation so you can be approved for other forms of business credit.

The second reason you might be declined is if you have shaky personal credit, which in turn is giving you fair-to-poor business credit scores.

If this is the case, you'll want to start off with easy to obtain tradelines like Nav.com, Shogun Roasting, The Red Spectrum, Business Apparel Club and Creative Analytics. You'll want to get a Credit Strong account, since this is a financial tradeline that reports to several bureaus. Again, it's all about building a really strong foundation so that you'll overcome deficiencies in other areas.

And if you are declined, you will either receive a written adverse action letter explaining that you were declined, or if you're on the phone with the credit department, they'll give you a verbal decline.

You can always ask for a reason why you were turned down; however, business lenders don't have to tell you why. To get the exact reasons, you must send a letter to the lender requesting a list of reasons for the denial.

What happens if I'm following the Pinnacle Score Pathway and I pay an invoice late?

In the personal credit realm, if you pay a credit card after the due date, you have a 30 day grace period before that late payment causes damage to your credit score.

You're NOT granted the same leniency in the business credit world! When it comes to business tradelines, your scores get wrecked if you're only one day past the due date. There is no grace period here. This is why I make such a big stink about paying your invoices early.

If you do end up paying a bill late, there's nothing you can do except continue using the Pinnacle Score Pathway and pay all new invoices early.

PART 3

How Lenders View
Your DOCUMENTS

Just like a builder wouldn't start a project without a set of blueprints, an entrepreneur should never seek funding without a well-organized dossier of documents.

Lenders can ask for documents at any point in the process, whether you're applying for a personal credit card or a million-dollar business loan. There's always a chance that you *may* need to submit specific documents with your application. (And notice I said 'may.')

The truth is, you can talk to 20 people who all got the same loan with no documentation; and then you go to apply, only to be met with a full-blown document inquisition.

It's nothing personal.

Financial institutions are required to follow the Bank Secrecy Act (BSA), specifically FinCen BSA/KYC requirements. The Bank Secrecy Act is a law that's meant to detect and prevent money laundering. KYC means Know Your Customer. This is all about banks performing due diligence before they provide you with an account.

All lenders have their own KYC compliance measurements in place. This is why they ask for identification like drivers licenses, passports, military ID, tax records, and so on.

According to the Financial Industry Regulatory Authority (FINRA), *"Every member shall use reasonable diligence, in regard to the opening and maintenance of every account, to know (and retain) the essential facts concerning every customer and concerning the authority of each person acting on behalf of such customer."*

And to take it a step further, financial institutions must also provide a periodic KYC refresh should they notice that you're engaging in activity that doesn't match your profile. Maybe you were labeled a Risk Level 1 when you applied. But two years in, your actions are screaming Risk Level 6.

This is the red-flag reason why a credit card issuer will suddenly ask for your tax returns or a 4056-T. If they notice that your spending/payment cycle suddenly increases, they may do a KYC refresh to make sure you're not doing anything that could put them in jeopardy.

Financial institutions that do not have a KYC compliance program in place, or those who are using it improperly, may be heavily fined. In 2022, almost $5 billion in fines were levied against financial institutions that violated BSA laws.

Besides BSA compliance requirements, you have to remember that when you apply for funding, certain parts of the underwriting are automated. When you get hit with a document request, it's usually because something in your credit profile or even your application automatically triggered the request.

After working with many Funding Preppers over the years, I know that when you're applying for personal credit or loans, you're more likely to be asked for documents if:

⊙ The income listed on your application is above a certain threshold. This could be in relation to the area you live in... income levels of those living in your area... and so on. For example, if you say you're making $150,000 a year, but you live in an area that's below the poverty level, this could trigger a documentation request.

⊙ You've lived at your current address for less than two years.

⊙ You're applying to certain credit unions, especially if they normally deal with a regional customer base, and you're well-outside of that geographical area.

⊙ The information on your credit report doesn't match what you've listed on the application.

Banks that offer business credit cards may ask for documents if:

⊙ They can't verify your business through your state's Secretary of State database.

⊙ You're a sole proprietor. Banks typically like to see that you're at least established as an LLC.

⊙ They want to verify your financials to establish a credit limit.

⊙ They want to see that your business makes enough to repay existing and new debt.

If you're applying for a business loan or a line of credit, you'll almost always need to provide documents. Once a loan request exceeds $1 million dollars, that document list will get even more extensive.

And while each lender has their own specific requirements, business loans that come from government backed sources (like the SBA), almost always require the most amount of documentation. That's because SBA affiliated banks can get into some serious hot water if they're consistently pushing through SBA loans that customers end up defaulting on. So, the banks have a real incentive for making you jump through the document hoop. Again, it's nothing personal.

In this section, you'll get a rundown of the many different types of documents lenders request... I'll explain why they're requesting it... and then for some of those documents, I'll tell you which type of lender will likely ask for it.

Think like a lender when preparing your documents

Welcome to Document-Palooza! This is a complete list of every document I've seen requested over the years. My suggestion is that you have the appropriate documents ready to roll out before you start applying.

The application process is far less stressful when you've got everything in hand, scanned, copied, and a click away from attaching.

- ⊙ **Driver's license/State ID**

  FUNDING TYPE: Personal credit card/loan, Business credit card/loan, line of credit

  PURPOSE: For identity and address verification. If the address on your application doesn't match your ID, you'll need 1-2 secondary forms of address verification. Make sure you have a PDF and a color fax-able version of this card - both front and back.

- ⊙ **Passport**

  FUNDING TYPE: Personal credit card/loan, Business credit card/loan, line of credit

  PURPOSE: For identity verification. If you have a passport, but no driver's license or state ID, you'll also need 1-2 secondary forms of address verification. Make sure you have a PDF and a color fax-able version of the first 2 pages. The signature must be seen.

- ⊙ **Military ID card**

  FUNDING TYPE: Personal credit card/loan, line of credit

  PURPOSE: For identity verification. Make sure you have a PDF and a color fax-able version of this card - both front and back.

⊙ **Social security card**

FUNDING TYPE: Personal credit card/loan, Business credit card/loan, line of credit

PURPOSE: For identity verification. Most likely you'll only be asked for a social security number. But depending on the lender and what's happening with your credit, you may be asked to submit a copy of the actual card. Make sure you have a PDF and a color fax-able version of this card - both front and back.

⊙ **Utility bill -- (Personal residence)**

FUNDING TYPE: Personal credit card/loan, Business credit card/loan

PURPOSE: For personal identity and address verification. If you're paperless, make sure you know how to download PDF versions of your bill. Sometimes business banks will ask for a utility bill if you're providing a passport for identity verification.

⊙ **Current lease or mortgage statement -- (Personal residence)**

FUNDING TYPE: Personal credit card/loan, line of credit

PURPOSE: For personal address identity and address verification.

⊙ **DD14**

FUNDING TYPE: Personal credit card/loan

PURPOSE: A DD14 is military discharge paperwork. Certain financial institutions only accept current/former military, or their immediate family members. For example, Navy Federal requires a DD14 to open an account if you (or your immediate family member) have been in the military.

⊙ **3 most recent pay stubs, if you're employed**

FUNDING TYPE: Personal credit card/loan, line of credit

PURPOSE: For financial and job verification. If a lender asks for your pay stubs and tax returns, they may cross reference the two documents to see if your tax return matches your pay stubs.

⊙ **Last 2 (possibly 3) years of W-2's**

FUNDING TYPE: Personal credit card/loan, Business credit card/loan, line of credit

PURPOSE: For financial and job verification. I recommend you use a service like ADP to issue you a paycheck every week. Even if your tax return shows self-employed income, it tends to be A LOT easier getting a personal loan or a credit card if you can show a W-2.

⊙ **Last 3 months' worth of personal bank statements where you receive direct deposits**

FUNDING TYPE: Personal credit card/loan, line of credit

PURPOSE: For financial and job verification. If you're paperless, make sure you know how to download PDF versions of your statement. Also keep in mind that many lenders now use Plaid to connect directly to your bank account, so they can see your direct deposits without paper statements.

⊙ **EIN**

FUNDING TYPE: Business credit card/loan, line of credit

PURPOSE: The Employment Identification Number (also known as the Tax Identification Number) is a 9-digit number that the IRS provides for your business. EIN's are required when you apply for business funding. It's also a necessity for opening a business bank account if your business is structured as an LLC, S-Corp, or C-Corp. (Make sure you download the PDF that the IRS provides with your EIN.)

⊙ **Business registration/DBA Filing**

FUNDING TYPE: Business loan, line of credit

PURPOSE: To confirm the legality of the business structure.

⊙ **Partnership agreement**

FUNDING TYPE: Business loan

PURPOSE: To confirm the legality of the business structure.

⊙ **Articles of incorporation/Operating agreement**

FUNDING TYPE: Business loan, line of credit

PURPOSE: To confirm the legality of the business structure if your business is registered as an LLC. The Articles of incorporation/Operating agreement is basically a framework outlining how your business will be run.

⊙ **Corporate bylaws**

FUNDING TYPE: Business loan, line of credit

PURPOSE: To confirm the legality of the business structure if your business is registered as an S or C corporation. This document may highlight info about the board of directors, members' responsibilities, as well as the overall structure of the organization.

⊙ **Last 3-6 months' worth of business bank account statements**

FUNDING TYPE: Business credit card/loan, line of credit

PURPOSE: Financial verification. If you're paperless, make sure you know how to download PDF versions of your statement. Also keep in mind that many lenders now use

Plaid to connect directly to your bank account, so they can see how much your business brings in without the paper statements.

⊙ **Last 1-3 years of personal tax returns, including all related schedules**

FUNDING TYPE: Personal credit card/loan, Business credit card/loan, line of credit

PURPOSE: Financial verification if you're employed or run a small business. Make sure you have PDFs of all the pages contained in your returns.

⊙ **Last 2 years of business tax returns, including all related schedules**

FUNDING TYPE: Business credit card/loan, line of credit

PURPOSE: Financial verification, if you have a C-corporation. Make sure you have PDFs of all the pages contained in your returns.

⊙ **Accounts payables**

FUNDING TYPE: Business loan

PURPOSE: Lenders may want to see a list of your current monthly debt payments to calculate how much funding you can comfortably afford to take on.

⊙ **A balance sheets**

FUNDING TYPE: Business loan, line of credit

PURPOSE: Details your assets and liabilities for a specific period, like January 1, 2023 - December 31, 2023. I recommend that you complete your balance sheet in a program like QuickBooks. (I'll explain why a little later in this chapter.)

- ⊙ **An income statements**

  FUNDING TYPE: Business loan, line of credit

  PURPOSE: Highlights what your company earns and what it spends. QuickBooks does this as well.

- ⊙ **A cash flow statement**

  FUNDING TYPE: Business loan, line of credit

  PURPOSE: Shows the amount of money that comes in and goes out of your business for a specific period of time, like January 1, 2023 - January 31, 2023. Yes... QuickBooks for the win again!

- ⊙ **Business license/seller's permit**

  FUNDING TYPE: Business loan, line of credit

  PURPOSE: If your business requires some kind of special permit or licensing, have the most recent copies available.

- ⊙ **Sales tax license**

  FUNDING TYPE: Business loan

  PURPOSE: This might also take the place of a resellers license.

- ⊙ **Loan application history**

  FUNDING TYPE: SBA 7(a) loan

  PURPOSE: To qualify for an SBA 7(a) loan, you must have been declined for a loan through other lenders. So, you'll need a list of other banks where you've applied to and the dates you applied. If you have the actual denial letters, even better.

⊙ **Vehicle title/registration**

FUNDING TYPE: Business loan

PURPOSE: If you have company vehicles that can be used as collateral, be prepared to show current titles and registrations.

⊙ **Name, address, telephone number and email address for your attorney, accountant, landlord, and life insurance agent**

FUNDING TYPE: Business loan

PURPOSE: Lenders may check your business records with intermediaries. You'll need to have these professionals on your team for higher limit loans exceeding $1,000,000.

⊙ **Life insurance policy binder**

FUNDING TYPE: Business loan over $500,000

PURPOSE: Some lenders require you to take out a life insurance policy that matches the amount of the loan you'll be receiving. You'll need to put the lender down as the beneficiary. This isn't common for small business loans, but once you start getting into the million-dollar range, it becomes more of a requirement.

⊙ **Business insurance policy binder**

FUNDING TYPE: Business loan over $500,000

PURPOSE: At minimum you'll need a general liability policy, business interruption insurance and business personal property insurance (also known as commercial property insurance). If the business owns real estate, you'll also need real estate hazard insurance. And if there are company vehicles, commercial vehicle coverage insurance.

- ☉ **Title commitment and insurance**

  FUNDING TYPE: Business loan

  PURPOSE: If you're providing real estate as collateral for a business loan, the lender may ask for an updated title search and title insurance commitment. An attorney may have to complete this part.

- ☉ **Property lease -- (Business)**

  FUNDING TYPE: Business loan

  PURPOSE: For certain business loans, your retail/plant/office space lease should be in sync with the term of the loan. For example, if the loan is for 4 years, your lease (including renewals) should also last for that long.

- ☉ **Real estate appraisal**

  FUNDING TYPE: Business acquisition loans, Commercial real estate loans

  PURPOSE: If you're purchasing commercial real estate, you'll need to have an appraisal done to determine if the loan requested is in sync with the value of the property.

- ☉ **Business plan**

  FUNDING TYPE: SBA loans, Business loans

  PURPOSE: Lenders want to see that you have a well thought out plan for growth. But most importantly, they want to know what you perceive as risks in your business and how you plan to mitigate those risks. You'll also want to make sure there's a professionally written bio for each member of your management team. It's important to outline the distinct qualifications and skill sets you have to run this business.

⊙ **Business valuation document**

FUNDING TYPE: Business acquisition loan

PURPOSE: If you need a loan to acquire an existing business, the lender will ask you for a valuation of the business. The SBA requires the valuation to be done by a third-party if the loan is over $250,000, or if the buyer and seller are related (family). For loans under $250,000 or those not covered by the SBA, the bank may have their own appraiser handle this process.

⊙ **Franchise documents**

FUNDING TYPE: Franchise loan, Business acquisition loan

PURPOSE: To give the lender information about the franchise you want to purchase. The franchise should already have documents that you can submit with your funding application.

⊙ **Client agreements/contracts**

FUNDING TYPE: Business loan, Business acquisition loan, Accounts receivable loan

PURPOSE: If you're asking for a loan based on your accounts receivables, you'll need to prove that you actually have those contracts.

⊙ **Outstanding invoices**

FUNDING TYPE: Accounts receivable loan, Factoring

PURPOSE: This is to show the lender how much money you need based on the accounts receivable invoices that have not been paid yet.

⊙ **Purchase agreement / Proforma**

FUNDING TYPE: Equipment loan, SBA 7(a) loan

PURPOSE: Shows lenders the final price of the equipment you're purchasing. The loan will be based on the amount listed in the agreement.

Think like a lender when looking at your bank statements

As you've already seen, both personal and business bank statements may be requested when you apply for funding. And depending on the lender, they may ask for paper copies of those statements, or to connect directly to your bank account through Plaid.

Often the priority is to verify your income, so the lender can provide a funding limit. But that's not all they're looking for. Bank statements provide black and white proof of your cashflow reality.

Lenders will look at them to see:

⊙ **How much cash you started with at the beginning of the month, and how much you had at the end of the month?** This is called the *opening and closing balance*. If you have a low balance from start to finish, a lender will instantly know that you're not ready for a business loan.

⊙ **What is the *average daily balance?*** The average daily balance tells lenders how well you're managing cash flow on a day-by-day basis. This metric is especially important to merchant cash advance lenders, since those loans are repaid on a daily or weekly basis.

⊙ **What is the source of income?** Where is the money coming from? For personal loans or lines of credit, they'll be looking for direct deposits from employers. And if you're a business owner who receives orders via credit card, they'll be looking for deposits from a credit card processor. They want to see how you're getting paid and where that cash is coming from.

Speaking of which, large cash deposits will never win you any favors with lenders. The main problem is that it looks like you're trying to artificially boost your numbers. Secondly, if it looks like it's a one-time occurrence, they won't even count it as part of your income/revenue.

⊙ **How often do you receive deposits?** The more often you've got deposits plopping into your account, the better. For example, if Stripe or PayPal is sending payments every day, you're likely in the safe zone (depending on how much you're receiving per order). But if you're not getting payments on a consistent basis, this could be seen as a red flag.

⊙ **What payments are being made?** Lenders are specifically looking for loan payments, credit card payments, and other monthly bills. This is all factored into your debt-to-income ratio and shows whether you have the capacity to repay a new loan.

⊙ **Do you have any overdrafts?** If you have more than 1-2 overdrafts a month, this could be a sign of poor cash management or impending struggles. Fortunately, it's an easily correctable situation. There should be zero overdrafts at least a couple months before you apply for loans and lines of credit.

⊙ **Do you have enough cash for an equity injection?** Some lenders (SBA lenders, in particular) will ask that you provide an equity injection on a business loan. What does this mean?

Suppose you're buying an existing business for $125,000. You would provide $25,000 from your own account and the bank would finance you for $100,000. That $25,000 you provide is the equity injection. Think of it as a down payment.

Lenders will look at your bank statements for the previous 2-6 months to make sure that you've earned the equity injection from the business. Equity injections shouldn't come from any loans, cash deposits or other funding sources.

All in all, this is about capacity. Do you have the *Capacity* to repay a new loan? (Hello again, 5 C's!) When capacity is on your side, it means you have the income to easily handle your existing debts, as well as a new loan.

Now let's look at some situations where bank statements may come into play during the funding process.

Bank statements for personal loans

During the pandemic, I got a $20,000 personal loan from a credit union where I had a $15,000 credit card and a savings account with $48 deposited in it. (Good credit is a wonderful thing!) I had only been a customer there for 3 months when I applied for the loan. It was an immediate approval. No bank statements were required.

A few weeks later, one of my Funding Prepper clients applied for the exact same loan. Even though his personal income was higher than mine, the bank ended up asking him for bank statements and a W-2.

I believe two things were happening here:

1) He had recently moved and the address on his credit report didn't match the address on the application.

2) His work income was above $400,000 a year. Listing a sizable income sometimes triggers a documentation request.

The interesting thing is that after all of that checking, he still got the same $20,000 loan offer. This is why I preach about having a solid financial profile, not just a good credit score or high income.

Bank statements for credit cards and lines of credit

Occasionally a creditor will ask you to submit bank statements before approving you for a personal credit card.

Before being approved for the X1 Visa, my client Alex (yes, the same Alex I talked about in *Think like a lender when looking at your existing business revenue*) had to connect his personal bank account using Plaid. X1 electronically checked his bank statements and ended up giving him a $22,000 limit.

I've been introducing Funding Preppers to a company called CarPutty. CarPutty provides lines of credit that you can use to buy new or used cars for business or personal use. Similar to the X1 Visa, they require bank statements through Plaid. That's how they determine the limits for the line of credit.

You'll find that certain credit unions require bank statements before they give you a credit card. I've seen this happen with smaller credit unions, especially if you're outside of their geographical region. And these smaller credit unions typically do not have automated approval, so their underwriters will manually go through your bank statements.

On the business side, American Express will sometimes ask for a 4056-T to verify your income if your spending is high, as compared to your stated salary. A 4056-T just gives them authorization to check your tax records through the IRS.

If a creditor requests it, it means they're trying to see if the salary you listed on your application matches your tax records. (This is why it's not recommended to lie on your applications.)

But if you have a new business and you're spending more than usual because business has suddenly started booming, they may take bank statements because your tax records probably don't corroborate your new spending pattern.

Lenders may not initially require bank statements. But if you don't have any other documents to support your claims, then a bank statement can end up saving you from a stressful account closure.

Bank statements for business loans

Business loans and bank statements are like peanut butter and jelly. If you're getting a business loan, you can be 100% assured that the lender is going to ask for business bank account statements.

The only time you're spared is if you're actively banking at the same financial institution where you're applying for the loan.

But if not, you may be required to give anywhere from 2-6 months' worth of statements. If a lender asks for more, it could be because you have a cyclical/seasonal business, and they want to see what your finances look like in the off months.

Think like a lender when looking at your tax returns

We know it's a possibility that lenders may ask for tax returns. But what is it that they're specifically looking for?

In a nutshell, tax returns show:

- That you have consistent income,
- Your income is verifiable,
- They show whether you have recurring income (income that has been received for 2+ years),
- And they show your business losses.

Out of all of this, lenders want to know that you have *significant, recurring income*. They are going to be looking at losses as well. But it's the significant, recurring income that makes-or-breaks the deal. This is true for both business and personal lenders.

Recurring means they want to see this income consistently appear on two or more tax returns.

So, let's say you started a food truck business in 2020. In early 2021, you also got a part-time job at Amazon. Then in November of 2021, you quit the Amazon job. Your 2021 income from Amazon was $18,340.

If you were to apply for a loan in 2022, the part-time job at Amazon would NOT be included as an income source in the lending decision. Why? Because you didn't have the job for more than 2 years. It's not *recurring*.

If you had that job in 2020, 2021, and you still have it in 2022, then yes... it would be considered a recurring income source, and it would be counted in the lending decision.

The food truck, however -- (because remember, you also had a food truck) -- would be counted as recurring income, if it appeared on your taxes in 2020 and 2021... and you're still running it in 2022.

Now let's look at it in another way.

This time you started the food truck business in 2019. In early 2020, you got a part-time job at Amazon. That job didn't have set hours. Your income depended on how many shifts you decided to take for the week.

In 2020, you made $1,211 at Amazon. In 2021, you made $1,590. You still have the job at Amazon in 2022 when you apply for a loan.

Even though this is recurring income for the past 2 years, it may not be considered *significant* income. In 2020, you earned $100.92 a month from Amazon. And in 2021, you only made $132.50 a month.

So, depending on the lender, this may not be enough to satisfy the *significant income* category, even though it's recurring.

Tax returns when applying for credit cards

If you're applying for a credit card, it's not likely that a lender will ask for tax returns.

I do find that this could happen if you're specifically targeting a credit card known for their high limits or picky standards. Smaller community banks and credit unions are also more likely to ask for tax returns... especially if you're not a long-time banking customer or you're outside of their geographic area.

Sometimes a bank will ask you to sign off on a 4056-T. Discover and American Express are known for their 4056-T requests both on the consumer and business side.

They will sometimes do this when your spending exceeds a certain threshold of your income. For instance, if you say your income is $75,000 a year, and you're spending $20,000 a month, this could automatically trigger a 4056-T request.

Even though you may be paying the bill several times a month to bring the balance down, they are known to be skittish about this sort of behavior.

In this case, it's best to be able to explain that maybe you have a new business that's not on your old tax returns. And then you'll need your business bank statements ready to corroborate the fact that you have a lot of new income coming in.

Tax returns when applying for business loans

If you're applying for a business loan, there's a 99% chance they'll require 2-3 years' worth of returns, including all the associated Schedules, for all owners of the business.

If you have a corporation or an LLC that's taxed like a corporation, and you file business taxes separately from your personal taxes, you'll need to show those returns as well.

SBA lenders require the previous 3 years of tax returns, including returns for the business itself, and returns for everyone who owns more than 10% of the business.

If you're consistently showing a strong profit on your taxes, you may be excited to give lenders those returns. What they find on those returns may allow them to give you a bigger loan than you anticipated.

With that said, if you have an accountant who *"works the numbers"* so that you'll pay the least amount of taxes, you may want to rethink that strategy. Downplaying your business profits on your taxes is THE WORST thing you can do if you want to successfully pursue funding in the future.

I've had SBA lenders turn clients away who could have easily gotten a beautiful, low interest loan, if they didn't play the business loss game into the ground.

If your business generated $200,000 last year, but your tax returns say you're only bringing home $40,000 a year, it's going to be extremely difficult to secure big money funding.

Not only that, if you ever want to sell your business, you don't want to make it look like a losing venture. And that means your tax returns must tell a certain story.

I won't wag my finger about that one too much. Just know that if you've been downplaying your profits for tax purposes, there's nothing you can do about it now. Let's just get that accountant on board for a better, stronger year this time.

Where will you find income on your tax returns?

Now that you understand the importance of recurring, significant income, let me show you where you'll find those amounts on your tax returns. In order to think like a lender, you'll need to tally the numbers just like a lender would.

Whenever you see a * next to an item, it means that the amount usually isn't included in the lending decision. Your situation may vary.

1040 - LINE 1: If you're employed, or receive tips, there will be income listed on line 1. Keep in mind, the lender will likely request copies of the last two years W-2's, and the 2 most recent pay stubs to prove that you're still employed.

*1040 - LINE 2A: This is tax exempt interest (for example, from municipal bonds). The lender may ask for a statement or deposit verification IF it is significant income. If it's not significant, it will not be included in the lending decision.

1040 - LINE 3A: Dividend income is reported here. You may be required to submit documentation or deposit verification.

1040 - LINE 4A: Shows non-taxed income from IRA distributions.

1040 - LINE 5A: Shows non-taxed income from pensions and annuities.

1040 - LINE 6A: Non-taxed social security benefits are listed here. This can include monthly, survivor or disability payments. SSI payments are not included here, because they're not taxable. And some disability payments may not be considered if it's not recurring income. The lender may require you to show an award letter or bank statements showing the deposits have been made.

* **1040 - LINE 7**: Shows capital gains and losses, from the buying/selling of stock, bonds, land, investment real estate or business properties. It only counts as income if you can prove similar transactions for the past few years. But if you sell your house and have capital gains here, it will not count as income, because it's not recurring. If you buy and sell houses every year, then it is counted as income.

1040 - LINE 8: This is where you'll list other sources of income that weren't included directly on the 1040. This would include business, real estate, and farming revenue (or loss), rental income, royalty payments, trust income, income from a partnership or an S corporation, unemployment, alimony or canceled debts. Since this includes business income, you must include a Schedule 1.

SCHEDULE 1

*SCHEDULE 1 - LINE 1: If you have any taxable refunds, credits, or offsets of state and local income taxes. This amount will likely not be included in the lending decision.

SCHEDULE 1 - LINE 2A: If you receive alimony, it will be listed here. It's typically not used in lending decisions unless:

- You want it to be considered for loan qualification,

- It makes a difference in whether the loan is approved or not,

- You can provide documentation that the support will continue, and for how long.

SCHEDULE 1 - LINE 3: This is where you include income from self-employment/small business. You should also have a Schedule C.

* SCHEDULE 1 - LINE 4: You'll list capital gains or losses from depreciable assets like real estate and business property/equipment. This is typically not recurring income, so it won't be included in the loan decision.

SCHEDULE 1 - LINE 5: If you have income/loss from real estate rentals, royalties, or you're a stockholder in a subchapter S corporation, or a member of an LLC, you would have income listed here. You should also have a Schedule E and/or Form K1 for these income sources.

SCHEDULE 1 - LINE 6: If you have income/loss from a farming operation it would show here. You would also have a Schedule F, which is used to determine farming cash flow.

* SCHEDULE 1 - LINE 7: This is for unemployment income. It's usually not included in the lending decision because unemployment is not considered recurring income.

* SCHEDULE 1 - LINE 8: Other income not listed elsewhere is included here, such as lottery/raffle winnings, prizes, gambling income, or awards are listed here at fair market value. These items are not included in the lending decision because winnings are not recurring.

SCHEDULE C

Should be completed by sole proprietors and single member LLCs, that file as disregarded entities.

SCHEDULE C - LINE F: If this is your first year in business, you'll need to decide between accrual and cash-based accounting. Small businesses usually go with cash accounting. But if you're an established business, and you've already used accrual-based accounting, then you have to stick with that. No flip-flopping on this one.

SCHEDULE C - LINE 7: This is your *gross business income*, which is calculated from amounts on Lines 1-6. It tells lenders how well you're doing sales-wise.

SCHEDULE C - LINE 31: One of the first lines analyzed. It shows *net profit* or loss, which is calculated by taking total revenue (or sales) and subtracting the total expenses. The amount shown is before taxes.

SCHEDULE E

If you have rental real estate income, royalties, partnerships, LLC or S Corporation revenue, you'll have to complete a Schedule E. (If any amount appears on Schedule 1, Line 5, then you'll need a Schedule E.)

Keep in mind that royalties do not pertain to book royalties here. Book royalties go on Schedule C. Royalties on Schedule E are from mining operations.

SCHEDULE E - LINE 3: If you have rental real estate, this line shows how much rent you received for the year. Lenders will see if there's an upward or downward trend from year to year.

SCHEDULE E - LINE 4: If you receive royalties from a mining business, when mining isn't a part of your main business, this is where you put the royalties.

SCHEDULE E - LINE 32: If you receive income from your role in a partnership or an S corporation, the total amount gets listed here. The lender may ask to see the K-1, which is issued to members (LLC) and partners and shows your share of the income or loss.

SCHEDULE E - LINE 37: If you receive income from a trust or estate, the total amount gets listed here. The lender may ask to see the K-1, which is issued to beneficiaries, and shows your share of the income or loss.

SCHEDULE F

Schedule F is similar to Schedule C, except it's specifically for farming income.

SCHEDULE F - LINE 9: This line shows the gross income from sales of: livestock/produce/grain and other items you raised, cooperative distributions, agricultural program payments, Commodity Credit Corporation (CCC) loans, crop insurance proceeds and federal crop disaster payments, custom hire (machine work), and other farming income that don't fit other categories.

SCHEDULE F - LINE 34: This is the net profit (or loss). The amount here is shown before taxes.

Think like a lender when looking at your financial statements

Maybe this will surprise you, (and maybe it won't...) but roughly 80% of the small business owners I talk to don't know a lot about financial statements.

Perhaps you've seen financial statements on QuickBooks. Maybe your accountant has given you a 12-month financial statement overview, and you've given it a one-minute reading. If so, you're doing good, because most business owners avoid them like the plague!

I used to be one of those people. Numbers just didn't excite me.

Growth excited me. Marketing excited me. Clients excited me. But in my head, financial statements felt like a wet blanket in a freezing cold room.

Today I see things much differently.

Why?

Because I experienced FAILURE!

When my bike shop failed, it was definitely because I didn't have any funding to cushion the business.

However, after really analyzing the situation, I also realized funding was a bandage that could only cover a piece of a bigger wound.

The bigger problem was that I knew how much I was spending, but I didn't realize how much real profit I was bringing in. Just because you have money in the bank, doesn't mean you're doing great. You could conceivably be heading towards bankruptcy AND have cash in the bank.

Understanding your business's financial health through financial statements can reveal problems that funding can really help solve. But even more important, financial statements can reveal situations where additional funding may not help you.

Yours may reveal that you need to use your existing cash flow in more productive ways, so that when you do get outside funding, you won't be using it in the wrong ways.

An overview of the financial statement universe

Here are the three financial statements you'll be working with.

   i.   Balance sheet

   ii.   Income statement

   iii. Cash flow statement

While lenders don't require these financial statements for personal loans, they may be a necessity for business loans, including all SBA loans, over $350,000. (Outside of the SBA, it really depends on the lender.)

I tell my clients that no matter how small your business is, you should always be keeping monthly financial statements. Not quarterly. Not yearly. Monthly. The end.

When you walk in with two years' worth of financial statements, it shows lenders that you keep good records. And that's usually a precursor to growth. Business owners who care about mitigating risk make them a less risky investment.

There are several reasons why lenders want to see your financial statements. Not every lender is assessing the same things.

   1.   **Financial statements are often used to determine the amount of the loan you're offered, as well as the terms, and the interest rate.**

2. **Financial statements tell lenders how well you're managing existing debt.** By looking at your income statement and your balance sheet, they can see what your debt-to-income ratio is. And as I mentioned before, the lower your debt-to-income ratio, the more equipped you are to take on more debt.

3. **Lenders may be trying to see if you have collateral.** Your balance sheet might show that you have real estate or specialized equipment.

4. **Financial statements tell the 'why' behind your numbers.** For example, if you say that you have $100,000 in assets and $30,000 in liabilities (debts), it looks like you have enough to support your operating expenses. But the balance sheet may show that your assets are broken down as $90,000 worth of inventory, $5,000 in equipment, and only $5,000 in cash.

   That is a very different funding situation than someone who has $10,000 in inventory, $20,000 in equipment and $70,000 in cash. So financial statements show the reality behind the numbers.

5. **Financial statements highlight revenue trends.** If you run a Shopify store, a lender is going to look at your income statements to see how your revenue changes during the slower seasons.

In most cases, small businesses are okay to submit *internally* prepared financial statements. This means you can fire up QuickBooks or any other do it yourself accounting apps and complete your own financial statements.

All you're doing is plugging in the numbers and QuickBooks creates the reports for you.

Plus (and this one is a little bonus item for Funding Preppers who are trying to decide on an accounting program) QuickBooks offers business loans to their users.

When you've reached a certain threshold in monthly income, you may receive an invitation to apply for a loan through QuickBooks. This is one of the better benefits of using QuickBooks over other accounting programs.

On the other hand, if you're requesting a loan over $2,000,000, then you'll want to get a CPA to prepare your financial statements. Why? Because it shows more credibility when you have a third-party handling your books, at that funding level.

How lenders view your balance sheet - Will you be able to pay your short-term debts?

The balance sheet shows a business's assets, liabilities and equity within a point in time, like March 1, 2023 - March 31, 2023. I always recommend that you complete a balance sheet on the last day of the month, this way you can make month-by-month comparisons throughout the year.

So first let's define what assets, liabilities and equity are.

A business's *assets* might include things like:

- Cash in the bank
- Accounts receivables (meaning money that's owed to you from clients)
- Inventory
- Prepaid expenses (like insurance you've paid in advance)
- Equipment
- Furniture
- Vehicles
- Buildings/real estate
- Patents, trademarks and intellectual property

Whereas *liabilities* may look like:

- ⊙ Loans (which is considered long term debt)
- ⊙ Credit card payments (which is short term debt)
- ⊙ Accounts payables (Money that you owe to others for products or services rendered)
- ⊙ Income taxes owed
- ⊙ Employee compensation (within the balance sheet's timeframe)
- ⊙ Utility costs

Equity is how much you have left over after liabilities are deducted from assets. Equity in the small business space is often called *owner's equity*, because it shows how much you can take home after everything is paid off.

The formula used to 'balance' the balance sheet goes like this:

Assets - Liabilities = Equity

Now, I'm giving you that formula just so you know it. However, lenders aren't looking solely at the raw numbers here. I mean *equity* isn't really the magic number they're looking for.

Lenders are crunching those balance sheet numbers into specific ratios to determine if you match their lending criteria. In other words, are your numbers within a comfortable level of risk for the lender?

Each financial statement has its own set of ratios. The balance sheet has four main ratios that small business lenders may utilize.

Debt-to-income ratio

The first one is the *debt-to-income ratio*, otherwise known as the *DTI ratio*. I gave you the personal DTI calculation in Part 1.

The debt-to-income ratio is a simple calculation that shows how much of your gross monthly income (gross monthly profits) is being used to pay down debt and loans.

It's calculated as such:

Debt / Income * 100 = DTI RATIO

Lenders use the DTI ratio to determine how much credit/money to extend to you. It's also one of the main reasons why creditors and lenders ask for your yearly income and the amount you pay for rent/mortgage on an application.

They can see how much debt you have on your credit report, and they're using an algorithm to guesstimate your monthly payments towards those existing debts. Then they're adding in the information you supplied about your mortgage/rent and dividing that amount by your yearly gross income.

When we talk about other debts included in this calculation, this includes:

- Vehicle loans
- Additional mortgages
- Credit card payments
- Loan payments

Debt-to-income ratio example

Peter's Pretty Plants is bringing in $18,000 in gross monthly profits. If Peter was also paying $6,000 towards monthly debts, his DTI ratio would be 33%.

6,000 (divided by) 18,000 = .33
.33 (multiplied by) 100 = 33%

SBA lenders like to see your DTI ratio below 40%-50%, depending on your overall credit profile.

In Funding Prepper land, that's too high. I recommend that you keep it below 20%-30% because that's where you tend to get better terms.

Don't get me wrong, it's okay to have debt, but you want to keep that debt at a level where you're able to slide through automated underwriting without any friction. The lower your DTI ratio, the better you're able to do that.

If you're looking for some simple ways to reduce your DTI, here's what I recommend:

1. **Negotiate lower interest rates on your existing debts.** For example, if you refinance the interest on your vehicle loan from 14% to 6%, your monthly payment will be lower. Even with the lower interest rate, I'd continue making the same monthly payment I had with the higher interest.

2. **Pay off a high-balance credit card (or two) before applying for a loan.** And I say this because I work with lenders who sometimes require clients to reduce or eliminate certain debts (like high balance credit cards) before they'll approve them for a loan.

3. **Keep in mind that owning investment property that still has a mortgage can add to your debt load, even if you're bringing in enough rental income to cover the monthly mortgage.** The mortgage can artificially inflate your debt even when it's not a liability.

   The key here is finding a lender that sees your investment property as a separate entity. Not every lender does this. But if you find one that does, your DTI ratio will appear more favorably, increasing your chances of getting a business loan.

Current ratio

Okay moving on... the second ratio lenders calculate on your balance sheet is called the *current ratio*, also known as the *working capital ratio*.

The current ratio shows lenders how easily you'll be able to pay off short-term debt. In other words, how quickly will your business be able to turn your current assets into cash, to pay off short-term liabilities.

And just so you'll understand what I mean by *current*, in accounting, *current* is anything that will be paid off or turned into cash within 12 months.

A credit card payment is a *current liability* because you'll make a payment every month. Your accounts receivables... money owed to you by invoice... are *current assets* because your clients will pay the invoice within 30 days.

The calculation for the current ratio looks like this:

Current Assets / Current Liabilities = CURRENT RATIO

Current ratio example

Peter sets up plant displays in office buildings. He secured 5 clients in June, and they were billed $10,000 each. Peter now has $50,000 in current assets.

Peter's Pretty Plants is also paying a mortgage on a commercial building where he has a storefront. He has 3 employees that he pays weekly. And then there's an American Express business card with a balance. It all totals up to $30,000 a month in current liabilities.

With $50,000 in current assets and $30,000 in current liabilities, Peter's current ratio is 1.7.

50,000 (divided by) 30,000 = 1.7

For a small business, a good current ratio is typically between 1.2 - 3.0. Peter has a current ratio of 1.7. He's in the safe zone.

Now suppose July rolls around and Peter only invoices 2 clients for $15,000 (current assets). One of his employees quits, but he still has $20,000 in debt (current liabilities).

His current ratio for July would be 0.75.

$$15,000 \text{ (divided by) } 20,000 = .75$$

A current ratio of less than 1 over several months shows lenders that your business isn't sustainable. The amount of money you're bringing in isn't enough to pay the monthly bills – or in accounting-speak, your current assets aren't covering your current liabilities.

While Peter may need funding at this point, lenders will see him as a risk. He won't get the funding he needs because he waited too long.

If you have an inventory intense business, (ecommerce, Shopify, Amazon, retail store) there's another ratio that some lenders prefer to use over the current ratio. It's called the *quick ratio.*

Quick ratio

The quick ratio (#3 on the list) is the same as the current ratio, but you subtract inventory from the equation.

It's a simple calculation:

(Current Assets - Inventory) / Current Liabilities = QUICK RATIO

Quick ratio example

Suppose Peter's Pretty Plants has $20,000 in current assets. $5,000 of that is cash in the bank, and the remaining $15,000 is inventory. (Remember, for the quick ratio, we're going to remove that $15,000 in inventory.)

Between his storefront rent, the loan for a hydroponics system, and the weekly pay for his employee, Peter has $6,000 in current liabilities.

His quick ratio would be .83.

$$20,000 - 15,000 = 5,000$$
$$5,000 \text{ (divided by) } 6,000 = .83$$

Similar to the current ratio, if your quick ratio is below 1, your business is viewed as a risk. Why? Because if you have a slow sales period, you'd be financially struggling to make it to the next month.

Look at Peter's numbers. All he needs is one bad month, and he'd have an immediate cash crunch!

Now let's look at it in another way. If Peter had $20,000 in current assets, with only $5,000 of that in inventory, and $15,000 in cash... and he still had those $6,000 in current liabilities, his quick ratio would be 2.5.

$$20,000 - 5,000 = 15,000$$
$$15,000 \text{ (divided by) } 6,000 = 2.5$$

A quick ratio between 1.2-2.5 means you're doing well. Peter has $2.50 in current assets for every $1.00 of current liability. He's in a comfortable position to handle short-term debt, with a little something left over for growth.

How lenders view your balance sheet - Will you be able to repay your long-term debt?

Now let's move on to the final balance sheet ratio, the *debt-to-equity ratio*, also known as the *debt ratio*.

If you're applying for a loan with a payback term that's greater than one year, this may be the ratio the lender uses. It determines your business's ability to pay long-term debts. (And just so you fully understand, as a small business owner, *equity* is how much you've personally invested into the business.)

Here is the calculation for the debt-to-equity ratio:

Total Liabilities / Equity = DEBT-TO-EQUITY RATIO

Debt-to-equity ratio example

If Peter's Pretty Plants had a $5,000 equipment loan for a hydroponics system, and another $5,000 in business credit card debt, he'd have $10,000 in total liabilities.

Separate from that, let's say Peter invested $4,000 of his own money into the business. That would the equity. In this case, Peter's debt-to-equity ratio would be 2.5.

10,000 (divided by) 4,000 = 2.5

A debt-to-equity ratio of 1 or more shows that your business is mainly funded by loans, lines of credit or credit cards. Anything under 1 means your personal equity is the primary funding source.

There's nothing inherently wrong with one side or the other. Remember, the startup phase is known for its rollercoaster ups and downs because newer businesses just naturally have more debt. Even highly successful startups may have a debt-to-equity ratio of 2 or more. So don't feel like you're doing something wrong if your debt-to-income ratio is a little high.

Your debt-to-income ratio becomes more of a deal breaker when it's viewed over the course of years. That's when lenders look at the debt-to-equity ratio by quarters, or sometimes years, to see if a business is trending up or down.

Before we move on, I'd like to point out that the debt-to-equity ratio is counted differently when it comes to SBA loans. The SBA calculates how much debt you have compared to the loan you're asking for.

For established businesses (two or more years) they allow for a 4.1 ratio, which means $4.00 of debt for every $1.00 of the loan. If you're a new business, it's a 3.1 ratio, which is $3.00 of debt for every $1.00 of the loan. The SBA gives you a lot more wiggle room than I suggest, but you still don't want to get so close to the edge.

How lenders view your income statement - Is your business as profitable as you say it is?

The *income statement* (known among accountants as the *net income statement* or *profit & loss statement*) details your business's revenue and expenses.

It tells lenders whether your business is making money, losing money or breaking even for a specific period of time, like March 1, 2023 - March 31, 2023.

The story of the income statement is told in 6 parts:

1. **Revenue:** Money made from the sales of your product or service.

2. **Cost of Goods Sold (COGS):** Labor and material costs for the goods you've sold.

3. **Gross Profit:** Revenue - COGS = Gross Profit

4. **Operating Expenses:** Salaries, utilities, lease payments, insurance, space rental, etc.

5. **Pre-Tax Profits:** Your business's total earnings before taxes.

6. **Net Income/Loss:** Total Revenue - Total Expenses = Net Income/Loss.

I won't get too technical with the accounting terminology here, but I should mention that there are two ways to do an income statement – *single-step* and *multi-step.*

A *single-step income statement* shows revenue and expenses, as well as profits or losses. If you're in the service industry, you sell a limited number of products, or you want to internally monitor the basics, then a single-step income statement is perfect. This is what we use for our hauling business.

A *multi-step income statement* does the same thing, except it separates operating revenue and operating expenses from non-operating revenue and non-operating expenses. It shows what revenue and expenses are directly tied to profit or loss. This means it takes longer to prepare than a single-step income statement, but it can also help you see precisely what needs to happen to become more profitable.

If your goal is to build a multi-million dollar business and sell it, then just get used to doing multi-step income statements. This is what potential buyers will ask for. I've seen a few Amazon FBA businesses get built up and sold off, and they always use multi-step income statements.

If you ever think you'll need $100,000+ in funding, you should absolutely be doing multi-step income statements. It shows lenders that you've got your eye keenly on the bottom line. It also provides them with the more granular details they'll need to make a decision.

When it comes to analyzing the numbers on an income statement, the *debt service coverage ratio,* or *DSCR* is the most popular. If a lender uses only one ratio, this is the proverbial "It" girl.

Debt service is the total sum of money your business owes to lenders, including both principal and interest payments. The DSCR tells lenders if you can comfortably pay your existing debt, and how much more debt you can afford to take on.

Although I suggest that you update your income statements every month, a lender who's calculating the DSCR will want to see yearly income statements. If you've been in business for 2-3+ years, they'll specifically be looking at how DSCR trends over time.

The formula for calculating DSCR is:

Annual Net Income / Annual Debt Obligations = DSCR

Annual net income is the amount of money your business makes selling products/services, NOT including your own salary, taxes, operating expenses and discretionary expenses (like a personal telephone bill, for example).

The *annual debt obligations*, which is the second part of the equation, is the total sum for a year's worth of funding debt and lease payments. Personal loans, business loans, business credit cards, vehicle loans, equipment leases, mortgages, lines of credit, and so on, are all considered to be annual debt obligations.

Debt service coverage ratio example

Peter's Pretty Plants had an annual net income of $100,000.

He was paying $435 a month for a vehicle loan. The annual debt obligation on that loan was $5,220 - (435 a month * 12 = 5,220).

He was also paying $1,365 a month on a line of credit. The annual debt obligation for that LOC was $16,380. His total annual debt obligation would be listed at $21,600.

Peter's Pretty Plants would have a DSCR of 4.63.

100,000 (divided by) 21,600 = 4.63

A DSCR greater than 1.25-1.50 is considered good, so in this situation, Peter's Pretty Plants would pass the DSCR test. The lender would know that Peter had 4x what's necessary to pay his existing debts and could conceivably take on more funding.

Now let's look at it another way.

Suppose Peter's Pretty Plants had $100,000 in annual net income, with an annual debt obligation of $85,000 a year. The DSCR would now be 1.18.

$$100,000 \text{ (divided by) } 85,000 = 1.18$$

Now that the DSCR is below 1.25, he may not get approved. The lender knows that for every dollar of debt Peter owes, he's bringing in $1.18. If he loses just 20% of business during a slow period, he won't have enough money to pay those existing debts. Clearly it doesn't provide much wiggle room for additional debt.

I mean even without doing any fancy mathematics, you can see that you're in the danger zone if your debts are almost on par with your income.

How lenders view your cash flow statement - Can you afford to take on a loan?

The *cash flow statement* (or *statement of cash flow*) is the last of the three financial statements. It tells lenders how much money is coming in and going out of the business within a specific period of time, like March 1, 2023 - March 31, 2023.

I like to think of the cash flow statement as the footnotes to the balance sheet. It provides a more detailed look at the multitude of factors creating revenue and loss within the business. It does this by specifically highlighting the cash that's coming in and the cash that's going out (known as *cash inflow* and *cash outflow*).

The cash flow statement shows lenders the real numbers.

If Peter says he sold $50,000 worth of plants in August, the cash flow statement might reveal that after everything was paid off, the business only had $5,000 in profit. That's a big difference.

Cash flow statements corroborate your story

Cash flow statements are the foundation for *cash flow projections*, which are necessary for SBA loans. In fact, you'll need to provide 12 months of cash flow projections when you apply for an SBA loan.

To do all this heavy lifting, the cash flow statement is divided into 3 sections:

1. **Cash flow from operations.** This is the cash you either earned or spent to operate the business. It could include cash you received from customers, as well as cash paid out to suppliers and wages paid to employees. When you pay rent, utilities, insurance, and taxes, it's all part of your operating expenses, which falls under cash flow from operations.

2. **Cash flow from investments.** In this setting, 'investments' could point to equipment or property that either costs or generates revenue for the business. (Remember, cash flow is all about money coming in AND money going out.)

   If you purchase a storefront, a warehouse or another piece of real estate for the business, that's an investment. If you acquire another business, that is also an investment. If you sold one of the $10,000 printers your business was using, that's also considered cash flow from investments.

3. **Cash flow from financing.** This is the net amount of cash that either comes in or goes out of your business from financing activities it's using. If you're currently paying on any loans, leases, or credit card debts related to your business, it's considered cash flow from financing.

We won't be using any ratios from the cash flow statement like we did with the balance sheet and the income statement. There are ratios I could provide; however, they're geared towards medium to larger corporations. Small business lenders are going to view the cash flow statement to pull raw numbers.

Lenders will look at your cash flow statements when they want to gather information like...

Why is there a significant jump in revenue? Is it because you sold an old piece of equipment on eBay... is it because you had a larger than usual sale that month... or is it because overall sales went up?

If revenue goes up because you sold an old piece of equipment on eBay, that's a non-sustainable one-time occurrence. Same thing if you're making large, non-typical sales on a periodic basis. But if you're doing the usual stuff and there's a steady upward trend, that's what they like to see.

Why is there negative cash flow? Negative cash flow isn't the end of the world. It's not unusual for a newer business in the startup phase to have periods of negative cash flow.

If you're investing in equipment that will help grow the business, that can be viewed as a good use of cash flow. You're spending money to make more money, even if it puts you in the negative.

If you're waiting for customers to pay 30-day invoices, this doesn't signify negative cash flow. But when customers are 60 or 90 days late, you've got a negative cash flow problem that stems from not collecting properly. That's not a good thing when you're looking for a loan. But if you want invoice factoring, then maybe that's something you can go for.

Preferably you should seek funding when you have positive cash flow. Still, you don't have to hide negative cash flow periods. If you're able to show why negative cash flow is a positive thing for your business at that time, you're still in the funding game.

PART 4

From "Figuring it Out" to Funded

Knowing what you need to get funded is the hard part. Well, at least it was the hard part. As of today, you can go into the application battle fully armed with enough knowledge to get all the approvals.

Now you're entering the 'search for a lender' phase, which can be an interesting challenge. The reason why applying for funding can be so stressful (especially when it comes to cash on the table), is because it can feel like a crapshoot when you're looking for a lender. If you do a search on Google, there are a gazillion lenders out there. It can be downright overwhelming.

And if you've ever applied for a loan and been denied, then you already know that a great sounding ad on Google doesn't always equal a positive experience. This is why I didn't provide names of specific lenders in this book. When it comes to niched funding options, it's rarely a 'one size fits all' situation. And on top of that, I would hate to recommend a lender here, only to have better options in my lender portfolio down the road.

Instead, I'm going to give you a more generalized route.

In this chapter, I'll introduce you to several different types of loans that you may not have known about. These aren't your typical, 'go-to-a-local-bank-and-get-a-loan,' products. These are niched funding options that work for a variety of unique situations.

I find that it's better to fully understand your own credit strengths, challenges and limitations before you look for a lender. Once you understand who you are, you'll have a good idea of what types of funding options could work for your situation. Then when you're searching for lenders, you'll know who's a good fit. This 'know thyself' approach limits denials.

However, even as you're limiting your options, you may still find the number of lending choices overwhelming.

This is where I excel. As a funding strategist, I handle that seeking out part for my clients.

I know what's out there. I know who offers great terms. I know who answers the phone, and who's backlogged. My up-to-date knowledge removes nuclear levels of frustration from your experience.

Lenders know that when I send in an applicant, they're smart about getting funded. My borrowers understand credit. They're not afraid to look risk in the face and mitigate the hell out of it. And with a book like this, they know the game from the inside out. This is what keeps everyone honest, happy, paid and repaid.

If you're interested, I provide a free 15-minute Pre-Funding Huddle. I can help you understand what the lending market looks like right now, for your credit situation. And we can start an application immediately. In many situations, I can get you funded in 24-48 hours.

In the spirit of transparency, let me say that it doesn't cost you anything up front to work with me. In some cases (not all) I do, receive a commission from the loan, once you receive the money.

I'm like a real estate buyers agent, in that I have a Rolodex full of lenders. But ultimately, I'm here to help you find what you need to be successful. If you're interested in a Pre-Funding Huddle, you can make an appointment at (FundedByMo.com).

Also, if you'd rather take a DIY approach, (LocateYourLender.com) is always an excellent starting point. This directory contains more credit cards and bank loans than the non-traditional funding options you'll find in this chapter. But it'll teach you how to find funding options that work for you.

Either way, you're ready to do this!

Use cashflow as your collateral

This is the funding option I've been talking about here and there throughout the book. The one where, Bad credit + Booming business cash flow = FUNDING!!!

I'm talking about merchant cash advances (MCA for short).

The amount you're offered is dependent on how much the business is bringing in – your cashflow. Just to give you an example, if you're bringing in $12,000 a month, you'll likely be offered anywhere from $3,000-$6,000 in funding, possibly more if your overall financial profile is strong.

This is not a loan. You're basically receiving an advance on the money you'd be making anyway.

Merchant cash advances are repaid on a daily, semi-daily or weekly basis. A specific amount will be automatically deducted from your business bank account -- like 10% of your daily income, or a flat amount determined by the lender.

When you apply for an MCA, the lender will ask for several things:

1) **You'll complete an application, detailing info about your business.**

   - What kind of business it is,

   - The structure... Whether it's an LLC, S-Corp or C-Corp,

   - The length of time you've been in business,

   - Amount needed,

   - Purpose for the MCA.

   (This is usually a one-pager, so don't worry about hairy details like profit and loss statements and that sort of thing.)

2) **3-6 months' worth of bank statements.** Obviously if you're attempting to get funded based on your business cashflow, the lender will need to see what that cashflow looks like.

3) **Credit card processing statements for the past 3-6 months.** Even though the credit card processor makes deposits into your business bank account, I recommend that you have these available anyway.

   Sometimes if you have a new merchant account, the lender may withhold a reserve from each sale. The statements themselves may show a bigger amount than what's being deposited into your bank account on a regular basis.

Minimum credit score accepted

550+

Types of businesses that get MCA funding

Merchant cash advances are specifically geared towards businesses that process credit card sales daily, like:

- ⊙ Retailers (online and offline)
- ⊙ Restaurants/Bars
- ⊙ Salons/Spas
- ⊙ Mechanics
- ⊙ Hotels/Lodging
- ⊙ Gyms/Fitness Centers
- ⊙ Local Service Businesses (landscapers, pool services, handyman, pet groomers, dry cleaners)
- ⊙ Membership Websites

How fast can you get funded?

1-2 days

Caveat

Bad credit does not do you any favors in the annual percentage rate (APR) department. So, if you have shaky credit, expect the APR rates to be higher than a traditional term loan, business loan, line of credit, or other traditional funding options. There's no way to dance around it.

The good part!

If you need to quickly stock up on inventory, this could be a good funding option for you.

If a vital piece of equipment breaks down, like the refrigerator in your restaurant, but you don't have the credit to buy something elsewhere... this is the funding option for you.

If you're having a short-term cash flow crunch, again with personal credit being a stopping point for everything else... this is what I recommend to you.

And best of all, MCAs do not report to your personal credit.

Home is where the money is

Your home is not only your castle, it's also one of the most widely used sources of collateral for business loans. I'm talking about Texas-sized business loans from $25,000-$2,000,000, depending on what kind of real estate you have in your portfolio and where it's located.

No... this is not a second mortgage. You won't be refinancing, nor is this a HELOC.

This is a business collateral loan that allows you to utilize your home (or almost any other form of real estate) as collateral. It doesn't matter if you've got a second mortgage... if you've taken out loans with other lenders... if you have existing merchant cash advances... or even if your business bank account has non-sufficient funds or negative days.

Your real estate equity and your business's revenue secures the loan. And by real estate, I mean a home (your primary residence in most states), vacation homes, apartment buildings, retail, industrial or commercial space, vacant or even agricultural land.

Think of a collateral loan as a step up from a merchant cash advance.

Both a merchant cash advance and a collateral loan are geared towards borrowers with fair to poor credit. Because of this, they both have higher-than-average interest rates.

An MCA will only allow you to borrow 40%-75% of your average monthly revenue. So, if you're bringing in about $50,000 a month, the maximum you can get with an MCA is around $20,000-$37,500 (give or take a few bucks).

A collateral loan is different in that you can borrow 100% of your average monthly revenue, provided you have the real estate equity to support it. This means if your business is bringing in $150,000 a month, and you've got a property worth $200,000, you could conceivably receive a $150,000 loan. (Yes, even with bad credit.) The payback period would be 12-18+ months.

To secure this kind of loan, you'll need six months of bank statements, and you must provide proof of real estate ownership.

Minimum credit score accepted

500+

Types of businesses that get collateral loan funding

- ⊙ Real Estate Investors
- ⊙ Seasonal Businesses
- ⊙ Online and Offline Retailers
- ⊙ Restaurants/Bars
- ⊙ Hotels/Motels/Airbnb
- ⊙ Construction Companies
- ⊙ Trucking/Transportation Companies
- ⊙ Business Service Providers

How fast can you get funded?

20-30 days

Caveat

Anytime you're using property as collateral, you risk losing the property if you default on the loan.

And on this type of loan, you may be required to make daily or weekly payments -- (which is similar to a merchant cash advance). Again, it depends on the terms of the loan.

The good part!

Because this loan is secured with collateral, you'll find that you won't need to supply certain documents like you would with a traditional unsecured loan.

Get funding for your tangibles

Just because a screwdriver is a tool, doesn't mean you should use it to hammer a nail into the wall. Not every tool is appropriate for every job. The same premise applies to funding.

It wouldn't make sense to get a $10,000 personal loan on your credit, when you could get $10,000 in equipment financing for that powder coating booth you've been eyeing – (and not have the financing show up on your personal credit).

Whether you need a conveyor belt, a reach-in refrigerator, a skid steer loader, an exam table, or any other major piece of equipment, equipment funding often ends up being a better choice than a regular loan or credit card.

Equipment lending comes in two different flavors, a loan and a lease. A loan allows you to keep the item once it's paid off. Having a lease means you can return the item or get an updated version after the lease term ends.

Startup businesses are often limited to how much they can receive. One lender I work with allows startups to receive $50,000 in equipment funding. And then once you have at least two years in the game, you'll qualify for $150,000 or more. Either way, the payback period varies from 12-60 months.

The lender is going to require an invoice for the item you'll be purchasing, in addition to an application and 3-6 months of your most recent business banking statements.

Minimum credit score accepted

580-680 (If your business is under two years old, you'll need a higher personal score, with home/property ownership.)

PAYDEX above 70

Types of businesses that get equipment financing

Funding can be provided for 'must have' equipment in industries, like:

⊙ Healthcare

⊙ Construction

⊙ Trucking, Transportation and Over the Road

⊙ Manufacturing

⊙ Restaurant

⊙ Computing

⊙ Retail

How fast can you get funded?

1-5 days

Caveat

Depending on the lender, your industry may or may not be covered for equipment financing. The lender mentioned above does not provide funding for anything that shoots, flies, floats or smokes. So, no guns, planes, boats or cannabis equipment.

Nonprofits funding for-profits

CDFIs are one of the least used sources for small business loans because most people don't know about them.

CDFI stands for Community Development Financial Institution. A CDFI is a bank, credit union or community development fund that provides money to underserved populations. This includes indigenous people, women, people of color, low/moderate income individuals, as well as those living in rural areas.

CDFIs are ideal if you have an existing business, but you've been denied a loan from a major financial institution. Some will require you to be in business for two or more years, or have industry experience. Others won't.

There's a growing list of regional CDFIs at (LocateYourLender.com), but in the meantime, let's take a look at Accion.

Accion is a CDFI that bills itself as the largest nationwide nonprofit lending network in the United States. This isn't one individual CDFI. Once you get in with Accion, they will refer you to the CDFI that makes the most sense for your situation. These CDFIs provide loans from $5,000-$250,000.

What I like about Accion (and most CDFIs) is that they focus on the big picture involved with running a business. They provide flexible repayment terms. They offer connections within the community. And some even offer educational services and technical support along with funding.

Each CDFI has its own requirements for application. I'm listing Accion's specifically since they're a nationwide organization.

- ⊙ Be no more than 30 days late on any bills, loans, credit cards, or any other payment. If you are late, the total late balance must be under $3,000.
- ⊙ Not have any mortgage-rate adjustments due during the term of the loan.
- ⊙ No bankruptcy filings in the past 12 months.
- ⊙ No late rent or mortgage payments in the past 12 months.
- ⊙ No foreclosures in the past 24 months.
- ⊙ Startups: Must have less than $3,000 in past-due debt.
- ⊙ Startups: Must present two most recent paystubs.
- ⊙ Startups: Have a business plan with a 12-month cash flow projection.
- ⊙ Startups: Have a partner referral (such as SCORE / SBDC)

Minimum credit score accepted

600+

Types of businesses that get CDFI funding

- ⊙ Women-owned businesses
- ⊙ Veteran-owned businesses
- ⊙ Native American owned businesses
- ⊙ Minority owned businesses
- ⊙ Businesses owned by low/moderate income earners
- ⊙ Businesses owned by disabled persons
- ⊙ Business owners in rural areas
- ⊙ Landscapers
- ⊙ Retail shops

⊙ Service businesses

⊙ Startups

⊙ Salons/Spas

⊙ Restaurants (Not solely bars)

⊙ Environmentally friendly businesses

⊙ And more -- just ask!

How fast can you get funded?

30-60 days

Caveat

Depending on the CDFI, you may get a UCC filing on your business credit report. The UCC filing shows other business lenders that you already have an existing loan.

The good part!

CDFIs aren't as credit score focused as traditional lenders. Having a low credit score isn't a cause for denial, but it might affect how much of a loan you receive.

From slow paying invoices to funds overnight

If you're a B2B or B2G supplier, you already know that even though it would be great to have all Net 15 accounts, larger corporations and government agencies can lean towards Net 30, 60 or even the dreaded Net 90, when it comes to paying your invoices.

And while that invoice is sitting pretty in payment limbo, employees, suppliers, rent, insurance and a myriad of other costs, still have to be paid. The business may be doing great on paper, but behind the scenes it may be struggling.

Fortunately, there's a bad-credit friendly lifeline available. It's called *invoice factoring*.

With invoice factoring, the lender agrees to buy your unpaid invoices at a 1%-6%+ discount. The factor amount usually depends on your industry and the level of risk involved, the stability of your business, the volume of invoices, amount per invoice, and your client's credit profile. Some factoring companies have a minimum invoice amount.

If you have bad credit, invoice factoring is great because your personal credit doesn't really come into play here. Lenders are primarily looking at the stability of your company, as well as the company that's paying the invoice.

The more reputable your clients, the better your chances of being approved for factoring. If you're selling to Fortune 500s, Fortune 1000s, or Inc 5000 companies, you should have no problems (unless the company has just announced they're having financial troubles). If you work under government contracts, that's ideal as well.

But if you're dealing with smaller companies that don't have well-established business credit, then you are likely to be denied. Factoring companies perform their due diligence before they'll approve a transaction.

Lastly, make sure that before you sign any contracts, you understand whether the lender provides *recourse* or *non-recourse* factoring. With recourse factoring, if your client doesn't pay the invoice, then you are responsible for repaying the factor. With non-recourse factoring, the factor assumes the risk if your client doesn't pay the invoice.

Minimum credit score accepted

580+

Types of business that get invoice factoring

- ⊙ Staffing/employment agencies
- ⊙ Janitorial services
- ⊙ Electrician/plumbing/utility services (Usually NOT construction)
- ⊙ Environmental services
- ⊙ Food/beverage
- ⊙ Distributors
- ⊙ Contractors/consultants
- ⊙ Transportation/logistics
- ⊙ Any other business that gets paid on Net 30+

How fast can you get funded?

1-2 days

Caveat

There are a few caveats here...

You will not be able to factor an invoice that's over 90 days old. I would suggest that if you're going to factor, you get started sooner rather than later.

Most invoice factoring lenders will require that you sign on for a minimum of 12 months. This means you must be willing to sell your invoices for at least a year. The tradeoff is that you'll have all your invoices immediately paid, allowing you to build your business onto a more solid financial footing.

And lastly, there are certain industries that factoring companies really don't touch. Construction is one of them. Medicaid/Medicare invoices is another. And you won't be able to factor invoices that come from a consumer.

The good part!

Some business owners raise their prices to compensate for the fact that they're invoice factoring. Feel free to make that idea your very own.

Funding you can use again, and again, and again

The older your business, the more funding options you tend to have. A business line of credit (BLOC) is one such option for businesses that are at least two years old and have a minimum yearly six-figure revenue.

Think of a BLOC as a hybrid between a loan and a credit card.

Like a credit card or a loan, you'll have access to a specific amount of money. But with a BLOC it's actual cash you'll have access to, instead of credit. Yet similar to a credit card, once you pay your BLOC debt, the cash is available for you to spend again.

It's a perfect option if you need a buffer for buying inventory or to avoid those slow periods that traditionally result in cash crunches.

Most major banks offer unsecured BLOCs. Though depending on the amount and the lender, you may have to use a CD (certificate of deposit) or real estate as collateral. For example, Bank of America requires either a blanket lien or a CD for business BLOCs over $100,000.

Minimum credit score accepted

650+

Types of businesses that get BLOC funding

Most businesses will be able to get a line of credit if you meet the credit score and monthly revenue requirements. Depending on the lender, some industries won't qualify. These might include transportation/trucking, real estate and construction.

How fast can you get funded?

1-2 days

Caveat

Business lines of credit are not for startups. Most lenders require that you've been in business for at least two years and have a minimum of $175,000 in yearly revenue.

PART 5

Using Personal Credit Cards and Loans for Business

I imagine you've picked up this book because the big goal is to get funding in your business name. But now that you understand the ABCs and 123s of it all, your current reality may look like a whole lot of funding in your personal name. At least for now.

If your business is a startup or your revenue is low, you may have to crawl with personal funding before you run with the business funding big dogs.

But as fate would have it, while you're walking the Pinnacle Score Pathway, computers die. Rock solid customers go out of business (before they pay you, of course). Suppliers run out of product. Government regulations change, forcing you to make drastic and expensive changes overnight.

Not everything can be anticipated. Not everything will be anticipated. (I use the COVID pandemic as exhibit one.)

And this is what sinks a lot of small business ships.

You may have all the education and experience in the world. You might have the hustle and drive of a thousand Gary Vaynerchuk's. But if you don't have the "in-case-of-emergency" stash of cash, there's a strong possibility your little LLC may end up D-E-A-D.

That's why I don't hesitate to recommend using personal loans and credit cards as a way to grow your business.

Don't get me wrong, tying up your personal credit isn't the most ideal situation. But as one of my elders used to say, "*Scared money doesn't make money.*"

In other words, you can sit on an idea until all your pretty little business credit ducks are lined up properly. But then you run the chance of watching someone else sprint off into Millionaire Land with your exact idea -- selling to the exact audience you had in your marketing plan. You know how life is. It's often very hilarious like that.

So instead of waiting for the most perfect circumstances, do whatcha gotta do, and do it the smart way. That's what this chapter is all about.

S-Corp and C-Corp Disclaimer

As I'm explaining the rules of the road, you'll notice that I've only focused on using personal funding in an LLC environment. That's because 99% of my clients' businesses are structured as LLCs. However, even if you have an S-Corp, you're going to find that many of the same rules apply. Just please check with an accountant if you're not 100% sure about what you're doing.

C-Corps... hmmmm not so much. C-Corps are very different animals and have unique rules regarding capital contributions to the business. For example, when you want to withdraw your capital contribution from a C-Corp, there could be an issue with double taxation. And that is beyond my scope of understanding, because I don't really have a huge C-Corp clientele.

I will, however, include some expert links at (FundingPreppers.com/BookLinks), so you'll have a better understanding of how to make this work for your C-Corp universe.

The power of an LLC

Like most LLC members or managers, you probably decided on this business structure because it protects your personal finances from being attacked if your company gets sued.

That's because an LLC is established as its own entity.

In fact, let's start thinking of an LLC as if it were a person.

If your (former) client Steve was to sue your LLC, technically he's not suing you. He's suing the entity (or identity) known as your LLC.

This is the simple strength of a limited liability corporation.

However, to achieve this limited liability protection, you'll need to maintain certain non-crossable boundaries between you and the LLC.

This is especially true when it comes to funding your LLC with personal money.

Things you CAN'T do with an LLC

According to the IRS, *"If a single-member LLC does not elect to be treated as a corporation, the LLC is a "disregarded entity,"* and the LLC's activities should be reflected on its owner's federal tax return."

This means that if you don't choose to treat your LLC like a corporation, the IRS will view a single-member LLC like a sole proprietorship. You'll file business taxes through your 1040, using a Schedule C, just as you would with a sole proprietorship.

And if you have a multiple-member LLC, the IRS views it the same way as a partnership. Each partner will file their business taxes using a 1040 and Schedule C, just like they would with a partnership business structure.

But that's where the similarities end. Just because the IRS views LLCs like a sole proprietorship or a partnership, doesn't mean you can run your LLC the same way a sole proprietor or a set of partners would.

For example, sole proprietors can mix and mingle business and personal funds in a single bank account because they are personally liable for any debt. It might be harder to figure out what's what during tax time, especially when it comes to deductions. But in the eyes of the IRS, the person who owns the business IS the business.

There's no limited liability with a sole proprietorship.

Because there's limited liability baked into an LLC, and because the LLC is a separate entity from the person(s) who started it, you cannot mix and mingle business and personal funds.

In fact, that's one of the biggest no-no's when it comes to running a business under the LLC structure.

If a check is made out to the LLC, you should not deposit it into your personal bank account. Likewise, if a check is made out to you, you should not deposit it into the LLC bank account. To do so is considered *commingling of funds*.

And it's this exact action that can get you into trouble if you're ever sued.

When you start commingling personal and business funds, it shows that the LLC isn't a separate entity from you. If you're ever sued, the opposing party's attorney will say that the LLC is your *alter ego*.

The *alter ego doctrine* allows the court to ignore your LLC's limited liability status and hold you personally liable for any debts your company incurs.

And if you also:

- ⊙ Fail to create and follow an operating agreement,

- ⊙ Neglect to initially fund the startup of the LLC,

- ⊙ Commit fraud (like take all the money out of the LLC bank account so you don't have to pay a creditor),

- ⊙ Treat the LLCs assets as if they were your own, ... you add more fuel to the liability fire.

The legal consequences of commingling

If your LLC gets sued and it's discovered that you've been commingling funds... never keeping cash in the LLC bank account... and you're not following the bylaws of the operating agreement, it may be ruled that you (not the LLC) are personally liable for any outstanding debts.

This is called *piercing the corporate veil.*

In this case, the judge will say that you're treating the LLC as your alter ego, instead of a separate entity. When that corporate veil is pierced, you no longer have the limited liability protection that an LLC traditionally gives you. Your personal assets can, and will, be taken if a judgment is filed against the business.

This is why it's vital that you understand how to keep your LLC in good standing, including how to fund your business properly.

An innocent mistake may not be a big deal if you never have any legal worries.

But if you ever need to defend the LLC in a court of law, you don't want to lose your house, your car, your retirement fund and everything you've worked so hard for, because you didn't take the time to understand how LLCs work.

This IS commingling of funds

⊙ Using a personal credit card to pay for business expenses.

⊙ Using your LLC's credit card to pay for your personal Netflix bill.

⊙ Having a single bank account for business and personal funds.

⊙ Depositing a check made out to you, into an LLC bank account.

⊙ Depositing a client check made out to the LLC, into your personal bank account.

⊙ Moving money between business and personal bank account without documenting the why's.

Contributing without commingling

I know all of that sounds scary, but there is a way to fund your LLC without potentially piercing the corporate veil. In fact, there are two options.

Let's start with *member contributions.*

You are considered a *member* of an LLC if you've provided funds to the startup and the running of the business, and your name is on the operating agreement. If you have a sole-member LLC, then you're considered a *manager* or a member.

As a member, you're allowed to provide *capital contributions* to the LLC, provided the operating agreement allows for it. And since you started the single-member LLC, and you've written the operating agreement, you have the right to allow capital contributions. Like I said, just make sure it's outlined in the operating agreement.

Multi-member LLCs must also make sure the terms of capital contributions are agreed upon by all members and outlined in the operating agreement.

Once your operating agreement allows for it, your capital contributions can take the form of:

⊙ Cash,

⊙ Services,

⊙ Tangible property (computers, vehicles, a building),

⊙ Intangible property (trademarks, domain names).

How capital contributions work

The first capital contribution you'll likely make is the cost of setting up the LLC.

Once the LLC is recognized by the Secretary of State, you'll open a bank account in the LLC's name. Then you'll make another capital contribution. This time, in the form of cash deposited to the bank account.

Although it's not required, I strongly suggest the LLC's bank account have enough money to handle the initial operating expenses for the business.

For a service business, this can be a few hundred dollars, maybe for a separate phone line and a website. When it comes to product businesses, think about how much you'll need for a starter supply of inventory, shipping supplies, etc.

That initial lump sum of funding you (and other members of the LLC) provide will help establish the legitimacy of the LLC as a separate entity. It shows that right from the start, the LLC has its own money.

Even if your LLC is a year or two old, it may not have started generating significant revenue. If this is the case, you might need to make additional capital contributions along the way.

For example, you could take $1,000 in cash, and deposit it into the LLC bank account. Or if the business needs a computer, you can purchase one on your personal credit card and give it to the LLC as a capital contribution. You can even take an existing asset, like a copyright, a trademark, or even an office building, and give it to the LLC as a capital contribution.

Now as you read those last few sentences, you might be thinking, *"Heyyyy... this all sounds like commingling of funds!"*

Actually, they all count as capital contributions, as long as you record the contributions in your accounting software (like QuickBooks) under *capital accounts.*

Capital accounts act as evidence against commingling

A capital account is simply an accounting notation. (It doesn't have anything to do with a bank account.)

Capital accounts are records of the financial activities that occur between a member and the LLC. This kind of paper trail proves the LLC was indeed its own entity. Without these records, it could appear that you're just commingling funds.

Even if you have a single-member LLC, you'll still need to record whatever transactions occur between you and the business. Remember, even though this is your business, the LLC is its own entity.

This means:

- ⊙ Whenever you make a capital contribution, be it cash or property, it gets included in the capital account.

- ⊙ When you receive a distribution (money from the LLC), that also gets recorded.

- ⊙ If a business loss is posted, that needs to be noted as well.

Even more important, make sure you're listing the reason why you made the member contribution. This is a big deal.

If you deposit $1,000 into the LLC bank account, make a note in your records that it was a capital contribution to replace inventory that was ruined in a flood... or to buy a new computer... or whatever it is you need to do business-wise.

(In the following section, I'll show you additional information that needs to be recorded for tangible and intangible property.)

Keeping capital account records is also a necessity for tax time.

Even though an LLC is reported on your 1040 (versus filing separate business taxes), keeping accurate records of what assets went where, keeps defined boundaries between personal cash and business revenue.

Your accountant will definitely appreciate this!

Adding non-cash contributions to a capital account

A non-cash contribution is anything a member gives to the LLC that has a cash value but isn't actual money.

Tangible contributions can include computers, office furniture, equipment, inventory, vehicles or land. Certain tangible contributions are deeded, like real estate. If you're still paying a mortgage to the bank, the bank may need to see that the LLC has strong enough credit before they'll transfer the deed to it. This is the only place where your business credit profile may be called in to testify.

Intangible contributions are things like copyrights, patents, trademarks, domain names, cloud-based software, memberships, or services. Basically, anything you can't physically put your hands on.

For both tangible or intangible property, you'll need to record:

⊙ **The actual price you paid for the item.** If you have a receipt, keep it for tax purposes.

⊙ **Fair market value (FMV).** FMV is the price an item would sell for right now in a competitive market. If an item has been purchased within the past couple of weeks, the FMV would likely be the price paid.

Another way to determine FMV is to see the price of comparable items. In this case, if I wanted to see how much an artist's print is worth on the open market, I would look on eBay for recent sales.

Professional appraisals may be reserved for real estate or specialty pieces of equipment, when seeking FMV for those items.

⊙ **Depreciated value.** Depreciation (for tax purposes) is when you take the price paid for the item and divide it evenly over a 5-year period. If you purchase a $2,000 computer, the depreciation would be $400 a year.

If that $2,000 computer is your capital contribution, and you've had it for 12 months, the depreciated value would be listed as $1,600.

Keep in mind, your accountant may calculate depreciation differently for your capital account.

⊙ **The reason why the transfer of property was made.** As I previously mentioned, you should always have a reason why you transferred cash or property to an LLC. This is done to show that LLC is not an alter ego, but an actual business entity.

Making loans to your LLC

The second way to fund your LLC is to make a loan to it.

And yes, this is possible even with a single member LLC. Since an LLC is a separate entity, a loan made to you is not the same as a loan made to the LLC. Conversely, a loan made to the LLC is not a loan made to you.

What this means is that if you get a $10,000 personal loan from your bank, you can then loan that money to the LLC.

(In this case, this is you – not the bank -- making the loan to the LLC. I just wanted to demonstrate how it's possible to use personal funding in a business situation.)

To do this properly, you'll need to create a promissory note for the LLC that outlines the exact terms of the loan, including repayment dates. You'll also need to charge the LLC reasonable interest on the loan.

If you take out a personal loan in your own name, and loan some or all of that money to the LLC, when the LLC pays the loan back, it will be paid directly to you.

The loan payment cannot go from the LLC to the bank where you got the loan. It has to go from the LLC to your personal bank account. Then you'll pay the loan back from your personal account to the bank.

I know this all seems formal, especially if you have a single member LLC.

But you have to treat the LLC as if it were an unrelated third-party, hence the need for repayment terms, interest and promissory documents.

Furthermore, make sure the LLC is making loan payments on time, and that you're recording the payments made and received (on the personal and business side) in your accounting software.

Should you have problems repaying the loan, the LLC's loan payment to the member cannot take priority over payments to outside creditors.

For example, if the LLC has a member loan with a repayment term of $100 a month, and a bank loan with a repayment term of $500 a month, the bank loan payment should be made before the member loan. Your personal equity in the LLC is always secondary to debt incurred from outside lenders.

When tax season rolls around, the loan will be counted as an asset to you, and a liability (debt) to the LLC. The loan is not tax deductible on your personal taxes. (This is why having an accountant on deck is necessary for these types of moves.)

Actions that do not count as commingling

I'll end this chapter by showing you some perfectly legal ways to contribute money to your LLC using personal loans or credit cards.

⊙ If you do not have personal credit cards that are designated strictly for business use, then use a credit card to purchase gift cards for the LLC. Now you can give those gift cards to the LLC as a capital contribution, allowing you to pay for business expenses using the gift card instead of a credit card.

⊙ If you want to pay your bills from LLC monies, you'll need to establish a monthly member draw or have the LLC pay you a salary. Pay your personal bills with that money. Never use your LLC debit card or bank account to pay your personal bills.

⊙ If you want to use your 9-to-5 work paycheck as a capital contribution, first deposit it into your personal bank account. Wait until it clears. Now take out the cash and deposit it into your LLC account. This can be noted in the capital account.

⊙ If a check is made out to the LLC, but you need it to pay personal bills, first deposit it into your LLC bank account. Wait until it clears. Now write a check to yourself from the LLC. That check can now be deposited into your personal bank account.

⊙ As long as it's mapped out in the Operation Agreement, this can be documented as a member draw, and it must be reported in the capital account as such.

⊙ Make sure you document EVERY transfer between your business and personal bank accounts as soon as you do it. You'll need this documentation for tax purposes and to prevent piercing of the corporate veil

PART 6

How to Keep Your Credit Profile Fully Optimized for Funding

You've just been given a 30,000 foot overview of all the behind-the-scenes details that go into the funding process.

My goal was to go above and beyond the basic information you'd find online. Therefore, some of the details you've seen in this book will apply to you, and some won't. Some will apply to you in one situation, and not another. In other words, you'll be prepared for anything.

More than that, I want you to stay prepared. I want you to woo-sahhhh into a state of perpetual financial profile perfection. This checklist will help you do just that.

This is not the end of the journey. This is the beginning of business growth beyond your wildest dreams. May success be eternally yours!

- ⊙ **Are you monitoring your credit reports from Experian, Equifax and Transunion at least once a month, and Innovis once a year?**

  You'll need to make sure that there are no errors on your credit reports. I recommend Experian.com for your three-bureau credit reports.

⊙ **Are your Experian, Equifax and Transunion FICO 8 scores all above 700 on a day-to-day basis? Above 720 during recessions and economic downturns? And above 760 for the highest possible limits?**

Knowing your personal credit scores is a must before you apply for both personal and business funding. You can get monthly access to your personal credit scores and credit reports at Experian.com. It's only $24.95 a month so you'll get the 3 bureau scores updated monthly.

⊙ **Do you have at least three tradelines on your personal credit with 18+ months of positive payment history?**

Both business and personal lenders prefer to see that you have a history of on-time payments. This is especially true if you're trying to get a loan.

⊙ **Do you have at least one personal credit card with a $5,000 limit?**

Non-bank lenders will want to see that your credit has been strong enough to support at least one average-limit credit card. This must be a Visa, Mastercard, American Express or Discover -- not a retail store card. See LocateYourLender.com for an ever-growing list of banks

⊙ **Do you know what's on your LexisNexis Consumer Disclosure report?**

Even though this report isn't widely viewed by lenders, sometimes it is checked for address verification or for high limit business loans. If there are errors in this report, some lenders will require additional paperwork to verify you.

⊙ **Do you know what's on your Accurint Comprehensive Report?**

This is also distributed by LexisNexis, and is used by lenders for asset identification, foreclosures and fraud. Again, you want to make sure that there are no errors on this report.

⊙ **Do you know what's on your CoreLogic Credco Consumer Report?**

CoreLogic Credco puts out a tri-merge report that's primarily used by mortgage and auto lenders. Make sure there are no errors on this report.

⊙ **Do you know what's on your ChexSystems Report?**

Banks use ChexSystems to see if you have overdrawn or bad accounts at other banks. Oftentimes credit unions will require you to open an account at their institution in order to get a personal loan -- and many of them do go through ChexSystems. So if you have any inaccuracies on your ChexSystems Report, you risk being shut out of many lending options.

⊙ **Have you ever defaulted on a federal loan?**

If you have any federally backed unpaid (defaulted) loans, foreclosures or liens, you're going to be in the CAIVRS (Credit Alert Interactive Verification Reporting System) database. This is an automatic disqualification for all SBA loans.

⊙ **Is your business bringing in at least $10,000 a month in revenue to a single bank account?**

This is usually the minimum I recommend for business funding. You can still get business funding if the business is bringing in less than $10,000, but your options/terms may not be as favorable. Also, the reason I suggest it all go into a single bank account is so that it's easily trackable through Plaid.

⊙ **Are you paying yourself a salary?**

Paying yourself a salary opens the door to more personal funding options. Having pay stubs shows personal lenders that you have consistent income, and it shows business lenders that the business is profitable.

⊙ **Do you know the risks associated with your industry?**

Depending on how much of a business loan you ask for, you'll need to be able to explain how your company can avoid those risks.

⊙ **Do you know what growth phase your business is in?**

Your funding options are dependent on whether you're in the startup, growth, mature or decline phase.

⊙ **Does your business have collateral that lenders can use?**

Collateral must have marketability, ascertainability, stability, transferability, durability and absence of liability. If it doesn't have all 6 of these features, it's likely not going to be accepted as collateral.

⊙ **Do you have at least 4-5 tradelines reporting on time to Dun & Bradstreet, Experian Business and Equifax Business?**

You will need at least 4 tradelines (accounts) reporting timely payments to all 3 of the business credit bureaus. You can always have more than 4, but that's the minimum if you want to qualify for or get higher limits on business credit cards and loans.

⊙ **Is your Dun & Bradstreet PAYDEX score at least an 80 or above?**

PAYDEX is one of your business credit scores that shows lenders how quickly you pay your business bills. You'll need at least 3 tradelines showing on-time payments to generate a score of at least 80. To get higher scores, you should be paying these accounts earlier.

- ⊙ **Is your Experian Business Intelliscore at least 75 or above?**

  This is one of your business credit scores that shows lenders how likely your business is to default on a payment within the next 12 months. You'll need at least 1 tradeline reporting for an Intelliscore to be generated. You can see yours at Nav.com.

- ⊙ **Is your Equifax Business score at least 450 or above?**

  The Equifax Business Delinquency Score predicts the likelihood of a business becoming delinquent within a 12-month time frame. You'll need at least 3+ tradelines reporting to start getting the best possible Equifax Business score.

- ⊙ **Is your FICO SBSS score 165 or above?**

  The SBSS is used by creditors and lenders to determine funding approvals and limits. The SBA requires you to have a 140 or above if you want an SBA loan. Most other business lenders require you to have a 160 or higher. Your SBSS score is built from both business and personal credit information.

- ⊙ **Have you collected all the necessary documents you'll need as outlined in the *Think like a lender when preparing your documents* section?**

  This list contains everything you'll need for any type of loan. You may not be required to give all these things, but it's good to have these things ready just in case.

- ⊙ **Have you calculated your ratios so that you'll know how much of a business loan you can comfortably afford?**

  This is all outlined in the *How lenders view your financial statements* section of this book.

- ⊙ **Do you have a list of potential risks your business could encounter?**

  This may not be a question on business loan applications. But this could be something that lenders verbally ask or look for in your business plan.

- ⊙ **Have you created a business plan?**

  Lenders that provide SBA loans will almost always require a business plan. Same with community-based microlenders.

- ⊙ **Have you created stellar management profiles for each principal in your business?**

  This is going to be a part of your business plan, and it's going to show how each person is qualified to be a part of your team. Emphasize degrees earned, previous positions held, and any major achievements as it pertains to your business.

- ⊙ **Do you have a LocateYourLender.com subscription?** This is where you're going to find application guidelines for banks, credit unions and other lenders. I've been building this directory since 2020 (Yup... it was my pandemic project.) These are guidelines contributed from Funding Prepper members who have been approved for credit cards, loans and lines of credit. Think of Locate Your Lender as the icing on the cake.

RESOURCES

FundingPreppers.com/BookLinks

All the sites I've mentioned in this book are listed and linked here.

FundingPreppers.com

My hometown. My dojo. The place in the cloud space where business owners never, ever worry whether they'll get approved.

While you're here, book a free 15-minute Pre-Funding Huddle. Bring your credit report and your credit scores, and I'll help you understand how to reach your funding goals.

Or get a copy of *Score More: 34 Ways to Improve, Maintain or Bring Your Credit Score Back from the Brink of Disaster (so you can get all the funding you want).*

LocateYourLender.com

If you've ever been nervous about applying for a credit card, a loan or a line of credit because you weren't sure if your application would be denied, then this is your happy place with a pizza on top.

Financial institutions normally do not reveal their underwriting guidelines. But that's okay, because members of Locate Your Lender kindly share the data behind their approvals and denials.

For each financial institution, you'll see which credit bureaus they use to run your credit, what scores you need to be approved, the maximum number of inquiries you should have, whether the offer hard inquiry or soft inquiry credit limit increases, and much more.

Made in the USA
Las Vegas, NV
18 March 2024

87323600R00125